JUST IN TI

WEDDING SERVICES

J. Wayne Pratt

Abingdon Press
Nashville

JUST IN TIME!
WEDDING SERVICES

Library of Congress Cataloging-in-Publication Data

Pratt, J. Wayne.
    Wedding services / J. Wayne Pratt.
        p. cm. — (Just in time!)
    ISBN 978-0-687-64888-7 (binding: perfect binding, adhesive : alk. paper)
    1. Marriage service. 2. Weddings. I. Title.

BV199.M3P73 2008
265'.5—dc22

                                                                    2008000147

08 09 10 11 12 13 14 15 16 17—10 9 8 7 6 5 4 3 2 1
MANUFACTURED IN THE UNITED STATES OF AMERICA

CONTENTS

Contents

ACKNOWLEDGMENTS

When invited to consider writing a book on wedding services as part of the Abingdon Press Just in Time! series, my first concern was how to tell the "old, old story" in a new, fresh, and invigorating way. I pondered some of the many words of wisdom that I have received from faculty members at Drew Theological Seminary. And so, a word of appreciation is certainly due to three caring and influential professors who have guided my journey in ministry. To Heather Murray Elkins who has offered encouragement and nurtured my attempts at creative writing and publication, I say thank you in a very large way. To my mentor and friend, Leonard Sweet, I am deeply indebted for teaching me to think, speak, and write using metaphors. His words of wisdom in and out of the classroom have been invaluable to me in so many different ways. And, to David Graybeal, who was always excited with and for me and my work, heartfelt thanks.

I am ever thankful for the unyielding support and encouragement offered from my wife—and partner in ministry and life—Becky. I really don't think any of this would be possible without the wisdom she has shared with me over the past ten years. Kind words are also extended to my aunt and uncle, Helen and Bill Schneider, for raising me when others were unable and to my late grandmother, Esther Leitner, for bringing me up in the faith.

To the members of Keokee Chapel and Wooddale United Methodist Churches, I would be totally remiss if I failed to say thank you in large measure for your encouragement and especially for your support during some very difficult times in the journey. You have stood by me, and for that, and so much more,

I am truly thankful. I have learned many valuable and important lessons with you.

My thanks also to Kathy Armistead at the United Methodist Publishing House, not only for extending the invitation to write this text but also for her faith in bringing a plebe into the publishing arena.

THANK YOU, ONE AND ALL!

INTRODUCTION

A wedding service is both meant and expected to be one of the most memorable experiences in a couple's life together. It is the sharing of a profound experience and the beginning of a wonderful journey in the most intimate of human relationships. A wedding is the joyful merging of the lives of two people whose friendship, understanding, and devotion to each other have flowered into romantic love. Marriage, then, is a lifelong commitment to share and grow into an even greater sense of intimacy, mutual trust, and friendship.

The wedding service is one of the most profound acts conducted by any church. It is a sacred event signifying the covenant made between two people, as well as between that couple and God. As such, it should be a worshipful experience in which a couple comes together seeking God's blessing. Since the church is a worshiping community rather than a building, a wedding service is much more meaningful when it is viewed as an extension of that community's ministry.

In the church wedding service the beauty, power, and majesty of God become dynamic hallmarks of the sacred occasion. Therefore, a wedding should never be thought of as simply a legal or social event and certainly not a performance. Any wedding service is first and foremost a worship service, an occasion to praise God and to seek God's divine power and peace in the years ahead.

Weddings are both a celebration of love and joy and a source of incredible stress. Those who officiate at wedding services are called to facilitate a ceremony that is reverent, joyful, and memorable. The pastor can also help alleviate some of the inherent stress that may be present.

In the United Methodist faith tradition, the *United Methodist Book of Worship* sets the standard for the conduct of services of Christian marriage. Today, however, couples seek to provide input into the design of their individual service and, conversely, pastors encourage couples to take a more active role in planning the wedding service liturgy.

With this in mind, pastors need to be aware that prospective wedding couples are increasingly searching the Internet for new and different resources for their wedding service. While many web sources provide vows, prayers, and other meaningful and appropriate wedding planning helps, some materials may be simply trendy and lack liturgical quality. Careful review of any resources provided by wedding participants is certainly encouraged before committing to their use.

This book offers an assortment of basic resources to the pastor in preparing for questions and difficulties that may arise, establishing policy statements regarding wedding services, and counseling couples in the design of their own unique service. Chapter 1, The Pastor's Basic Toolkit, provides an overview of local legal requirements, church and pastoral policy information forms, music guidelines, and other considerations involved in the preparation for and conduct of wedding services. Chapter 2, Wedding Service Components, offers model service material covering each of the basic components of the wedding ceremony, including vows, prayers, blessings, readings, and other materials. Chapter 3, Wedding Meditations, provides a variety of basic wedding homily and sermon materials that can be readily adapted to individual circumstances and settings.

Each and every wedding service presents the pastor with a unique opportunity to witness to the love of God present in the world today, to extend a greater sense of hospitality to the unchurched or *dechurched*, and to open new and exciting doors or *entry points* into the life of the church. A wedding that is truly memorable to the bride and groom, their families, and the gathered assembly, is both tailored to the couple's needs and offers a high degree of personalization. The music, words, and actions of all involved certainly aid in creating an environment of welcome and comfort. In essence, wedding services may, to a certain extent, be regarded as a means of outreach, aimed at touching people's emotions, souls, and lives.

It is the intent of this volume to provide a spark for pastors to engage in the development of creative liturgies and to make each wedding service a truly memorable occasion for all involved. May you find joy and inspiration in this volume and may it serve to facilitate your ministry of creating and employing meaningful wedding liturgies.

CHAPTER ONE

THE PASTOR'S BASIC TOOLKIT

Every pastor needs to maintain a basic toolkit of selected resources that will aid in the preparation and conduct of wedding services. Documented information on local legal requirements, church and pastoral policies, fees, forms to be completed, and general wedding guidelines will greatly assist in expediting efforts and will serve to alleviate stress, miscommunication, and issues concerned with legal and procedural matters. Likewise, a ready reference of service-oriented liturgical resources is a valuable necessity.

LOCAL LEGAL REQUIREMENTS

Specific marriage license requirements differ from state to state, and even from county to county. Generally speaking, however, a valid license may usually be obtained from the county clerk's office or a county records department. Some local jurisdictions have established a separate marriage license bureau to process applications and disseminate documentation. In other jurisdictions a town clerk or similar officer may be empowered to issue such licenses.

One of the first deliberate actions a pastor should take is to search out the local legal authority that processes marriage licenses and become familiar with local and state laws that regulate their issuance. While securing the marriage license is the responsibility of the couple, there are times when a couple may ask for a pastor's assistance in locating the proper authorities, or seek information on waiting time requirements, fees, residency requirements, or minimum age stipulations. Primary questions in the application process and issuance of marriage licenses most often deal with age of consent, residence and citizenship requirements, the dissolution of any previous marriages, the necessity of blood test results or other health information, necessary identification, and fees required.

Following the wedding ceremony, the pastor is required to sign the wedding certificate for the couple. A legal form often attached to the wedding certificate and certifying the marriage must also be signed and returned to the proper authorities. Many jurisdictions note that failure to return this signed document may result in a fine; therefore, prompt processing is necessary.

Names, addresses, and phone numbers of marriage license contacts in the community and surrounding area will prove invaluable over the course of one's ministry.

CHURCH WEDDING POLICY STATEMENTS

In order to avoid undue confusion, hard feelings between pastor and church administrators, and miscommunication with the prospective bridal couple, churches need to have set in place well-defined policy statements for the conduct of weddings. Such statements should, at the very least, address issues such as use of the church, membership requirements, fees associated with such use by members and nonmembers, use of outside clergy and musicians, decorations, and general expectations regarding personal conduct, post-service cleanup, and other similar issues.

The Church Policy Statement should be shared with and explained to the couple during the initial meeting at which wedding arrangements are discussed.

PASTOR'S POLICY STATEMENTS

Every pastor should also formulate a basic statement of policies concerning the conduct of weddings. The policy statement serves to answer many of the basic questions that may arise when a couple asks you to perform their marriage ceremony. The policy statement needs to be supportive of any church policies that are in place. The Pastor's Policy Statement should be shared with the wedding couple during the initial contact. See a sample policy statement in appendix B.

INTERFAITH MARRIAGES

The number of interfaith marriages is certainly on the rise. Social and cultural barriers that once hindered or even prevented many couples from marrying are now being bridged. At times, a pastor may be requested to perform a wedding in which the bride and groom are of different faith traditions. The pastor must carefully consider and be sensitive to a host of issues that may arise in such circumstances. Likewise, the pastor, in concert with the couple, needs to carefully consider appropriate readings, the wording of vows, and other materials that will be included in the ceremony. Cultural and ethnic traditions and customs also need to be discussed in advance of the ceremony, as their inclusion can aid in creating a much more meaningful ceremony. The inclusion of appropriate cultural and ethnic components affords a greater sense of validity to the couple, their families, and the guests present.

SECOND OR SUBSEQUENT MARRIAGES

While marriage is intended "until we are parted by death," divorce rates are increasing at dramatic rates. Divorce can be defined as the unfortunate rupture or breaking of a promise or covenant. It is a painful but sometimes unavoidable tragedy that deeply affects many families. Because Christians trust in God's mercy and the human capacity to be healed and made whole, divorce does not generally bar anyone from entering into a new marriage covenant.

Premarital counseling will greatly assist the pastor in determining that individuals are sufficiently aware of the factors that contributed to the failure of the previous marriage. Likewise, appropriate counseling will assist in ensuring that no unresolved conflicts or "baggage" are brought into the new marriage. One factor to consider is that appropriate time has passed since the divorce, allowing the couple to freely consider their new life together.

The death of spouses, at various ages, and the desire of widows and widowers to remarry create unique opportunities for wedding services. Some people who remarry after the death of a spouse may be concerned that any mention of death will have a negative impact on their celebration, especially if children are to be part of the wedding service. As with any wedding, the pastor must be sensitive to the issues at hand.

While the previous marriages of one or both partners may, at times, present challenges to the pastor, weddings of this kind are also an opportunity to create a very meaningful and creative ritual in the lives of the couple. Portions of the ceremony should address such unusual circumstances by incorporating children from the previous marriage(s) into the liturgy. Examples of such inclusion are illustrated in chapter 2.

WEDDING INFORMATION FORMS

One of the basic administrative tools a pastor can use is a Wedding Information Form. This document will serve to assemble

4

and centralize a host of information regarding the wedding couple, service arrangements, and other vital information, which may be needed for future reference. Information requested on the form should be collected during one of the initial counseling sessions held with the couple. See appendix A for a sample Wedding Information Form.

BASIC MUSIC GUIDELINES

Music can be a major element at a wedding, which often does not receive sufficient attention. Just as other elements (location, dress, flowers, liturgy, and décor) are crucial in setting the tone for the event, music offers a unique way to convey the feelings, emotions, and personalities of the couple and the theme of the service. Music is an important means to help guests relax and become comfortable as they wait for the service to begin. Music has the ability to set the mood, evoke emotion, and provide a measure of cohesiveness and continuity.

It cannot be stressed enough that all music must be discussed with the instrumentalist and pastor as an integral part of the overall design of the service. Many wedding couples today seek to include trendy, popular music as a part of the service. The wedding, however, must be viewed, first and foremost, as a worship service with music selections appropriate to the occasion. Church organists and music ministers are capable of offering suggestions for the selection of appropriate music to be used for preludes, processionals, recessionals, and postludes. Traditional and classic selections are numerous. Likewise, several contemporary offerings may be deemed appropriate. The following presents a basic listing of service music that may be appropriate for the wedding service.

Prelude Selections

- "Adagio" (from *Sonata in E-Flat*), by Mozart
- "Air" (from *Water Music*), by Handel

- "Air on a G String" (from *Orchestral Suite, no. 3*), J. S. Bach
- "Allegro" (from *Brandenburg Concerto no. 4 in G*), by J. S. Bach
- Nocturne in E-Flat, Opus 9, no. 2, by Chopin
- "Waltz" (from Act 1 of *Sleeping Beauty*), by Tchaikovsky

Processional Selections

- "Traditional Wedding March" (from *Lohengrin*), by Wagner
- Trumpet Tune, by Purcell
- "Trumpet Voluntary" (from *Prince of Denmark's March*), by Clarke
- Canon in D, by Pachelbel
- "Romance" (from *String Quartet*), by Mozart

Interlude Selections

- "Jesu, Joy of Man's Desiring," by J. S. Bach
- "Air on a G String" (from *Orchestral Suite, no. 3*), J. S. Bach
- "Ave Maria," by either Schubert or Gounod
- "Ode to Joy," by Beethoven

Unity Candle Selections

- "Jesu, Joy of Man's Desiring," by J. S. Bach
- "There Is Love (Wedding Song)," by Noel Paul Stookey
- "Ave Maria," by Schubert
- "Amazing Grace," by John Newton
- "Flesh of My Flesh," by Leon Patillo
- Canon in D, by Pachelbel
- "You Light Up My Life," by Joe Brooks

Recessional Selections

- Traditional "Wedding March" (from *A Midsummer Night's Dream*), by Mendelssohn

- "Ode to Joy," by Beethoven
- "Spring" or "Autumn" (from *Four Seasons*), by Vivaldi
- Sonata in G, by Tartini
- "Toccata" (from *Organ Symphony no. 5*), by Widor
- First Movement (from the *Brandenberg Concerto no. 1 in F*), by J. S. Bach

Again, coordinating music between the wedding couple and musicians is of utmost importance and should be accomplished early in the wedding planning process. Professional musicians will certainly be able to expand on the above list and offer the couple a greater variety of selections to choose from. Input from the wedding couple also helps to personalize the service so it will be remembered as a joyous, fitting event in the life of the couple and those who gather for such a momentous occasion.

CHAPTER TWO

WEDDING SERVICE COMPONENTS

While most religious denominations provide basic guidelines regarding the structure and content of the typical wedding service, there is a growing trend to personalize much of the liturgy to fit the unique setting, the couple's desires and faith experience (or lack of experience), and the context and culture of the worshiping community. While denominational guides are certainly the pastor's first line of reference and need to be consulted and shared with the couple, alternative vows, prayers, readings, and other resources can also be considered. Following is a basic selection of resources that may be employed in the formulation of the wedding liturgy. It is presented as a supplement to denominational resources. Included here are numerous alternative options for each element of the wedding service as well as information on many newer, more innovative liturgical components.

In addition to those listed here, a wealth of resources can be found on the Internet by typing keywords such as *wedding, marriage service,* or *wedding liturgies* into your browser search window. You will find a vast array of prayers, poems, romantic readings, and alternative rituals. Be judicious in using these resources. Review them carefully for appropriateness and compatibility with your denominational needs. Also be aware that Web materials often lack source or copyright documentation.

The resources included in this book are certainly not exhaustive in scope, but every attempt has been made to provide the seed for additional creative enterprise on the part of the pastor. Use the presented materials as a basis for further refinement and adaptation in personalizing the occasion for each couple. The presentation of resources follows the typical order of service for a religious wedding.

PROCESSIONAL

Often the question arises as to the proper order for families to be seated and the wedding party to process to the altar area. The following is a summary of the typical order.

1. The guests are seated. Generally, looking from the back, the bride's family and friends are seated on the left and the groom's family and friends are seated on the right. This need not, however, be strictly observed.
2. The groom, best man, and officiate enter and take their places.
3. An usher escorts the grandmother(s) of the bride to their seats.
4. An usher escorts the grandmother(s) of the groom to their seats.
5. An usher escorts the mother and father of the groom to their seats.
6. An usher escorts the mother of the bride to her seat.
7. Processional music begins.
8. The bride's mother (and father, if seated) stands.
9. All the guests stand.
10. Ushers walk down the aisle (or escort the bridesmaids), stand next to the groom and best man, and face the congregation. The usher standing farthest from the groom enters first.
11. The bridesmaids walk down the aisle. The bridesmaid standing farthest from the bride enters first.

12. The maid/matron of honor walks down the aisle.
13. The ring bearer walks down the aisle.
14. If a runner is to be used, this is the time to unroll it.
15. The flower girl walks down the aisle.
16. Processional music changes and/or the volume increases.
17. The father of the bride (or other presenter) escorts the bride down the aisle.

While numerous variations may be possible, it is wise to coordinate any necessary changes or modifications to the typical order with the wedding couple prior to the scheduled rehearsal.

GATHERING

During the Gathering, prior to the actual start of the wedding service, special instrumental or vocal music may be offered. The music ultimately selected by the wedding couple aids in setting the mood for service; it is played while guests are arriving and the congregation is assembling. When the service is ready to proceed, the processional music itself will commence. Some wedding couples may request that an anthem or solo be presented at this time rather than the traditional organ or keyboard selections.

All music to be presented in the wedding service should be coordinated with the church musician and pastor to ensure an appropriate selection of materials. As noted earlier, pop tunes and trendy music should usually be avoided; the music offered during the Gathering helps sets the stage for a worshipful church experience.

GREETING

The primary purpose of the Greeting is to extend cordial words of welcome to the congregation on behalf of the couple and their families, and to state the basic meaning and purpose of the ceremony. It is also an invitation to corporate and holy worship. A short prayer, if desired, may precede or follow the Greeting.

Prayers before the Greeting

Prayer (option 1)

Lord God,
we are gathered in your loving presence
 to celebrate the marriage
  of *(Bride's Name)* and *(Groom's Name)*.
We ask your blessing as they exchange their vows
 and enter into a life as husband and wife.
Fill them; fill all of us with your Spirit
 that we may be the image of your love
  in the world today.
Look upon them and look upon us with your favor
 that we may rejoice and give thanks. Amen.

Prayer (option 2)

O God, we gather to celebrate not only the gift of love
 but also your presence among us.
We thank you for the ways you have touched the lives
 of *(Bride's Name)* and *(Groom's Name)*.
Renew within each of us
 an affectionate spirit and caring attitude.
May our sharing in this celebration of love
 give to us a newfound sense of faith and joy.

Prayer (option 3)

Loving God,
you have created man and woman for each other;
let your blessing be upon this couple as they
pledge themselves to each other.
We ask this in Jesus' name. Amen.

ᶜ **Greetings**

Greeting (option 1)

Family members, friends, children of God:
we are gathered together on this solemn occasion
   to witness and bless the marriage
      of *(Bride's Name)* and *(Groom's Name)*.
We affirm that marriage is truly a gift from God;
   a gift that is sealed by an act of sacred covenant.
With our love, prayers, and fellowship,
   we support without reservation
      (Bride's Name) and *(Groom's Name)*
   as they freely offer themselves
      in this marriage covenant.

Greeting (option 2)

This is the time that *(Bride's Name)* and *(Groom's Name)*
   have chosen to become husband and wife.
We are gathered not only to witness
   your commitment to each other
but also to wish you both joy, peace,
   and happiness in your future together.
Within the framework of commitment and loyalty,
   your marriage enables the establishment of a home,
      where, through patience, trust, and mutual respect,
   the love and affection which you now share
      with one another
   may truly develop into a deep and lasting relationship.
We who are witnessing your marriage covenant
   hope and pray that, despite the stresses
   that often accompany life's journey,
   your love and respect for one another,
   your trust and understanding of each other
   will increase your contentment and heighten your joy.

Greeting (option 3)

On behalf of *(Bride's Name)* and *(Groom's Name)*
  and their families
I welcome you to this service of worship.
This gathering is both a sacred ceremony
  and joyous festival
    in which we all have a part.
Today, this man and this woman are here
  to publicly give their marriage vows to each other.
We are here both as witnesses to these vows
  and to celebrate with husband and wife
  their love and affection for one another.
In the journey of life; in the final accounting,
  love and the search for love
  are what life is all about.

Greeting (option 4)

Dear friends, we gather in the presence of God
  to witness the marriage
  of *(Bride's Name)* and *(Groom's Name)*,
  to share in this their day of great joy,
  and embrace them with God's grace and peace.
We remember that marriage is a gift from God,
  a sacred and holy act of covenant.
With our love, our thoughts, our prayers,
  we honor and support
    (Bride's Name) and *(Groom's Name)*,
  as they freely give themselves to each other.

Greeting for Renewal of Vows

Family members, friends,
we are gathered together at the invitation
  of *(Bride's Name)* and *(Groom's Name)*
  as they reaffirm their wedding vows.

(Bride's Name) and *(Groom's Name)* celebrated their
    union in marriage on *(date of wedding)*.
God has richly blessed this couple
    and in their continuing love for one another,
    they reaffirm a covenant that they hold near and dear.
Let us worship God together.

CHARGE TO THE COUPLE

The Charge to the Couple has at its basic core the general pos-
ing of the question regarding the couple's free and mutual decision to enter into the covenant of marriage. The Charge
essentially serves as an introduction to the Declaration of Intent
and Consent that follows. The words of the Charge serve to
remind the couple of the serious nature of the covenant they are
about to confirm; the vows they are about to exchange should
not be taken lightly, but rather should be offered in a spirit of
honesty and integrity.

Charge (option 1)

(Bride's Name) and *(Groom's Name)*,
I ask you now, in the presence of God
    and these people (or, this congregation),
    to declare your intention to be united in holy marriage
    through the grace and love of Jesus Christ,
        who calls you into union with himself
        as acknowledged in your baptism.

Charge (option 2)

Before God and these people,
I ask you to state your willingness and desire
    to enter into this marriage
    and to share with one another
    all that life has to offer.

Charge (option 3)

I charge you both, as you stand in God's holy presence,
   to declare your intention to enter
      into the covenant of marriage.
If the vows you are about to exchange are given in faith
   and you strive to do the will of God,
your lives will be full of joy, and your home
   a haven of peace.
Surely no other ties are more sacred
   than those you now offer
   as you seek to bind yourself to each other.

DECLARATION OF INTENT

The Declaration of Intent forms one of the minimum basic legal requirements of a valid marriage ceremony and asks the individuals individually and specifically about their desire to be married, and often includes the obligations of one partner to the other.

Declaration of Intent (option 1)

(Groom's Name),
   will you have *(Bride's Name)* to be your wife,
      to live together in holy marriage?
Will you love, comfort, honor, and keep her,
   in sickness and in health, and forsaking all others,
   be faithful to her as long as you both shall live?
Groom: I will *(I do)*.

(Bride's Name),
   will you have *(Groom's Name)* to be your husband,
      to live together in holy marriage?
Will you love, comfort, honor, and keep him,
   in sickness and in health, and forsaking all others,
   be faithful to him as long as you both shall live?
Bride: I will *(I do)*.

Declaration of Intent (option 2)

(Groom's Name),
> will you have (Bride's Name) to be your wife,
> to be your partner in life, your friend, your mate,
> and will you love her faithfully
>> as long as you both shall live?

Groom: I will (I do).

(Bride's Name),
> will you have (Groom's Name) to be your husband,
> to be your partner in life, your friend, your mate,
> and will you love him faithfully
>> as long as you both shall live?

Bride: I will (I do).

Declaration of Intent (option 3)

Do you (Groom's Name), take (Bride's Name)
> to be your wife;
> and do you promise before God, your families,
>> and this gathering,
to be a loving, loyal, and faithful husband to her,
> as long as you both shall live?

Groom: I do promise.

Do you (Bride's Name), take (Groom's Name)
> to be your husband;
> and do you promise before God, your families,
>> and this gathering,
to be a loving, loyal, and faithful wife to him,
> as long as you both shall live?

Bride: I do promise.

Declaration of Intent (option 4)

(Bride's Name) and (Groom's Name),
I ask you now in the presence of God
> and this gathering,
>> to state your desire to enter into marriage,

to be a true and faithful partner,
pledging your faith to one another,
    according to the will and grace of God.
Groom: I so desire.
Bride: I so desire.

PRESENTATION

Parents and other family members often play an important part in a wedding ceremony. Several options for the Presentation of the bride are available and appropriate for the wedding service. The once-traditional phrase of "given in marriage" has largely fallen out of favor in recent years and should be avoided. While this role of Presentation typically falls to the father of the bride, both parents, children by a former marriage and other alternatives exist. Increasingly, both parents of the bride make the Presentation.

Presentation (option 1)

Pastor: Who presents this woman to be married to this man?

Presenter: I do. (*Her mother and I do. We do.*)

(*The groom may also be presented. In such cases the following would be appropriate*)

Pastor: Who presents this man to be married?

Presenter: I do (*His mother and I do. We do.*)

Presentation (option 2)

Pastor: Will the parents of the bride and groom please stand?
Who is bringing (*Bride's Name*) to be joined in marriage to (*Groom's Name*)?

Bride's Parents: We are.

Pastor: Who is bringing (*Groom's Name*) to be married to (*Bride's Name*)?

Groom's Parents: We are.
     Pastor: Are you willing now and always to support and strengthen this marriage by upholding both (*Bride's Name*) and (*Groom's Name*) with your love, your concern, your counsel, and your prayers?
All Parents: We are.
     Pastor: Thank you. You may be seated.

Presentation (option 3)

     Pastor: As (*Bride's Name*) and (*Groom's Name*) today become husband and wife, they leave their families to create a new one. As you have held them close and dear, shaping their lives to maturity, will you now release them to love and care for each other? And will you, the families of this couple, pledge to them the continued love and support they need?
All Parents: Yes, we will.

(Following the Presentation, it is appropriate that parents or representatives of the families of the bride and groom come forward to light the candles that will later be used in the Unity Candle Ceremony [if used]. A token of thanks is sometimes offered by the bride and groom to the mothers at this point in the service. A rose for the mothers or some other symbol will add meaning to the service.)

MOTHERS' ROSE PRESENTATION

A simple, yet very powerful and perhaps very emotional, offering at the conclusion of the Presentation is the gift of a rose to the mothers of the bride and groom. A small vase with two roses is placed on the altar prior to the wedding service. At the conclusion of the Presentation, the bride and groom each remove a rose from the vase, and together they move to where the mother of the bride is seated and present her with a single rose. They then move to the mother of the groom and do likewise. Following are suggestions for introductory words for this symbolic gesture. It should be noted that some wedding couples prefer the rose presentation to be a surprise to the mothers with no introduction offered. In such cases, it may be possible to offer the explanatory words following the presentation.

Modify the words of introduction appropriately if fathers, grandmothers, children, or other significant family members are included in this offering of thanks.

Suggested Introduction to Mothers' Rose Presentation

Marriage is the coming together of two individual lives and a celebration of the love that this couple shares. However, it is much more than that. The precious gift of love that *(Bride's Name)* and *(Groom's Name)* share for one another is the flowering of a seed their parents planted in their hearts many years ago. As they embrace one another in love, so they also embrace the families that have brought them together on this joyful occasion. As a sign of their love for their respective families, *(Bride's Name)* and *(Groom's Name)* offer these gifts to their mothers.

(Bride's Name) and *(Groom's Name)* desire that you know your love for them is very much appreciated. They thank you for all that you have instilled in them. It can be said that these roses are a gift, a promise that no matter how far apart you may be, you will always be in their minds and hearts.

RESPONSE OF FAMILIES, CHILDREN, AND CONGREGATION

The Response of the Families, Children, and Congregation serves to publicly declare an affirmation of the marriage and to convey a sense of mutual support. While not always included in the service, the Response does have the potential to offer a broader sense of incorporation into the families of the wedding

couple. It may take the form of a responsive liturgy or simply con-
sist of an offer to those gathered to convey words of support and
encouragement.

Response (option 1)

Pastor: The marriage of (Bride's Name) and (Groom's
Name) unites their families and creates a new
one. (Bride's Name) and (Groom's Name) ask
for your blessing upon this marriage.
Do you, the representatives of their families, affirm
this union and pray God's blessing on them?

Families: We do.

(If there are children by former marriages, the children may respond.)

Children: We love you both and pray for God's blessing.
Together we will be a family.

Response (option 2)

Pastor: Will the families of (Bride's Name) and
(Groom's Name) please stand. This marriage
brings together a variety of family histories, traditions, and ideals. Theirs is truly a personal
choice, yet their lives together will certainly be
enriched by the support of their families. And
so, parents, I ask these questions of you:
Do you celebrate with them the decision
they have made to choose each other?

Families: We do.

Pastor: Do you affirm your support and unconditional
love to (Bride's Name) and (Groom's Name) as
they grow together in marriage?

Families: We do.

Pastor: Will you offer to them the best of your care
and counsel in their times of struggle and will
you celebrate with them in times of joy and
accomplishment?

Families: We will.
Pastor: Thank you. You may be seated.

Response (option 3)

Pastor: That couple is truly rich that enters into marriage with the blessing of family and friends.
Will you, the parents of (*Bride's Name*) and
(*Groom's Name*) now give to them your blessing and pledge to them your continued love
and support? Will you share your experiences
and wisdom with them in a loving and caring
manner? Will you be sensitive to their needs,
their desires, and their hopes and dreams? If so,
please respond, we will.
Families: We will.

OPENING PRAYER

The Opening Prayer is offered as a means to define the importance of the ceremony as a service of God-inspired worship, as
well as a wedding service. The prayer typically invites God's presence, gives thanks for the wedding day, and seeks a divine blessing for the wedding couple.

√ Opening Prayers

An Act of Faithful Covenant

Gracious and almighty God,
 we praise you for your presence with us,
 and in this act of faithful covenant.
Look with grace upon
 (*Bride's Name*) and (*Groom's Name*)
 who stand before you and seek your blessing.

Offer to them your love and your grace
    as they now begin their journey through life together.
Enrich their lives with the gift of your Holy Spirit
    that they may be nurtured and sustained in a love
    that also knows no bounds.
In Jesus' name we pray. Amen.

A Prayer for Steadfast Love

Gracious God,
you have always been faithful in your love for us
    and so we rejoice in your presence this day.
You embrace us with the precious gift of your love;
    a love that is given without reservation,
    without condition, without expectation.
May our participation in this celebration
    give us a renewed sense of peace and joy.
Let your Holy Spirit dwell within them
    so that with steadfast love
    they may honor the vows they make this day,
through Christ Jesus our Lord. Amen.

Prayer in a Garden Setting

Loving God, Creator of us all,
    from our beginnings in Eden's garden
    you have willed our love to be fruitful.
In this garden setting today,
    with the beauty of your creation surrounding us,
    we are keenly aware of your divine presence.
Bind *(Bride's Name)* and *(Groom's Name)*
    in this gift of marriage
    so that their journey may be filled with
    the beauty of a constantly flowering love.
Bless all your creation and unite us in a garden of grace.
Fill this couple's hearts with truth and beauty
    as they share in this act of holy covenant. Amen.

A Loving and Faithful God

Loving God,
    ever faithful in your love toward us
    we rejoice in your presence and your promise
    to embrace us with compassion and care.
Look now, dear Lord, on
    (Bride's Name) and *(Groom's Name)*,
    as they stand before you and share
        the blessing of their love.
Bless them as they pledge their lives and beings
    to one another in this celebration of marriage.
May the power of your Holy Spirit sustain them
    and all of us in the perfect love that you offer.
In Jesus' name. Amen.

For a Renewal of Vows

Loving and Caring God,
    what a joy it is to see a couple so deeply in love
    that they choose to reaffirm that which is good.
We ask your continued blessing
    on *(Bride's Name)* and *(Groom's Name)*
    as they renew the marriage vows they first exchanged
    (number of years) years ago.
They come with a spirit of thankfulness
    and we, too, are thankful for their lives among us.
Bless them this day, O Lord, and in all their days to come.
We pray this in Jesus' precious name. Amen.

SCRIPTURE READINGS

One or more passages from Scripture may be read by the pastor, a member of the wedding party, a family member, or other layperson. The reading of sacred Scripture serves as a Christian witness to God's affirmation of love and marriage. Other appropriate readings from literature or poetry may be read in addition to a biblical passage.

The following is a brief array of suggested passages of Scripture that are suitable for the typical wedding service. In every case, however, the wedding couple should be asked if they have any favorite passages that they would like to have shared during the service. The inclusion of such passages, if appropriate, lends to the personalization of the service. The following passages are from the New Revised Standard Version of the Bible.

Genesis 1:26-28, 31—The Creation of Man and Woman

Then God said, "Let us make humankind in our image, according to our likeness; and let them have dominion over the fish of the sea, and over the birds of the air, and over the cattle, and over all the wild animals of the earth, and over every creeping thing that creeps upon the earth."

So God created humankind in his image, in the image of God he created them; male and female he created them. God blessed them, and God said to them, "Be fruitful and multiply, and fill the earth and subdue it; and have dominion over the fish of the sea and over the birds of the air and over every living thing that moves upon the earth."

God saw everything that he had made, and indeed, it was very good.

Genesis 2:4-9, 15-24—Becoming One Flesh

These are the generations of the heavens and the earth when they were created. In the day that the LORD God made the earth and the heavens, when no plant of the field was yet in the earth and no herb of the field had yet sprung up—for the LORD God had not caused it to rain upon the earth, and there was no one to till the ground; but a stream would rise from the earth, and water the whole face of the ground—then the LORD God formed man from the dust of the ground, and breathed into his nostrils the breath of life; and the man became a living being. And the LORD God planted a garden in Eden, in the east; and there he put the man whom he had formed. Out of the ground the LORD God made to grow every tree that is pleasant to the sight and good for food, the tree of life also in the midst of the garden, and the tree of the knowledge of good and evil.

The LORD God took the man and put him in the garden of Eden to till it and keep it. And the LORD God commanded the man, "You may freely eat of every tree of the garden; but of the tree of the knowledge of good and evil you shall not eat, for in the day that you eat of it you shall die."

Then the LORD God said, "It is not good that the man should be alone; I will make him a helper as his partner." So out of the ground the LORD God formed every animal of the field and every bird of the air, and brought them to the man to see what he would call them; and whatever the man called every living creature, that was its name. The man gave names to all cattle, and to the birds of the air, and to every animal of the field; but for the man there was not found a helper as his partner. So the LORD God caused a deep sleep to fall upon the man, and he slept; then he took one of his ribs and closed up its place with flesh. And the rib that the LORD God had taken from the man he made into a woman and brought her to the man. Then the man said, "This at last is bone of my bones and flesh of my flesh; this one shall be called Woman, for out of Man this one was taken."

Therefore a man leaves his father and his mother and clings to his wife, and they become one flesh.

Proverbs 3:3-6—Trust and Honor God

Do not let loyalty and faithfulness forsake you; bind them around your neck, write them on the tablet of your heart. So you will find favor and good repute in the sight of God and of people.

Trust in the LORD with all your heart, and do not rely on your own insight. In all your ways acknowledge him, and he will make straight your paths.

Isaiah 63:7-9—The Steadfast Love of the Lord

I will recount the gracious deeds of the LORD, the praiseworthy acts of the LORD, because of all that the LORD has done for us, and the great favor to the house of Israel that he has shown them according to his mercy, according to the abundance of his steadfast love. For he said, "Surely they are my people, children who will not deal falsely"; and he became their savior in all their distress. It was no messenger or angel but his presence that saved them; in his love and in his pity he redeemed them; he lifted them up and carried them all the days of old.

Jeremiah 31:31-34—A New Covenant

The days are surely coming, says the LORD, when I will make a new covenant with the house of Israel and the house of Judah. It will not be like the covenant I made with their ancestors when I took them by the hand to bring them out of the land of Egypt—a covenant that they broke though, I was their husband, says the LORD. But this is the covenant that I will make with the house of Israel after those days, says the LORD: I will put my law within them, and I will write it on their hearts; and I will be their God, and they shall be my people. No longer shall they teach one another, or say to each other, "Know the LORD," for they shall all know me, from the least of them to the greatest, says the LORD; for I will forgive their iniquity, and remember their sin no more.

Matthew 5:13-16—Salt and Light

"You are the salt of the earth; but if salt has lost its taste, how can its saltiness be restored? It is no longer good for anything, but is thrown out and trampled under foot.

"You are the light of the world. A city built on a hill cannot be hid. No one after lighting a lamp puts it under the bushel basket, but on the lampstand, and it gives light to all in the house. In the same way, let your light shine before others, so that they may see your good works and give glory to your Father in heaven."

Matthew 19:3-6—Jesus' Teaching on Divorce

Some Pharisees came to him, and to test him they asked, "Is it lawful for a man to divorce his wife for any cause?" He answered, "Have you not read that the one who made them at the beginning 'made them male and female,' and said, 'For this reason a man shall leave his father and mother and be joined to his wife, and the two shall become one flesh'? So they are no longer two, but one flesh. Therefore what God has joined together, let no one separate."

Matthew 22:34-40—The Greatest Commandment

When the Pharisees learned that he had silenced the Sadducees, they gathered together, and one of them, a lawyer, asked him a question to test him. "Teacher, which command-ment in the law is the greatest?" He said to him, " 'You shall love the Lord your God with all your heart, and with all your soul, and with all your mind.' This is the greatest and first com-mandment. And a second is like it: 'You shall love your neigh-bor as yourself.' On these two commandments hang all the law and prophets."

Mark 10:6-9, 13-16—No Longer Two, but One

"But from the beginning of creation, 'God made them male and female.' 'For this reason a man shall leave his father and mother and be joined to his wife, and the two shall become one flesh.' So they are no longer two, but one flesh. Therefore what God has joined together, let no one separate."

People were bringing little children to him in order that he might touch them; and the disciples spoke sternly to them. But when Jesus saw this, he was indignant and said to them, "Let the little children come to me; do not stop them; for it is to such as these that the kingdom of God belongs. Truly I tell you, whoever does not receive the kingdom of God as a little child will never enter it." And he took them up in his arms, laid his hands on them, and blessed them.

John 2:1-11—A Wedding Feast at Cana

On the third day there was a wedding in Cana of Galilee, and the mother of Jesus was there. Jesus and his disciples had also been invited to the wedding. When the wine gave out, the mother of Jesus said to him, "They have no wine." And Jesus said to her, "Woman, what concern is that to you and to me? My hour has not yet come." His mother said to the servants, "Do whatever he tells you." Now standing there were six stone water jars for the Jewish rites of purification, each holding twenty or thirty gallons. Jesus said to them "Fill the jars with water." And they filled them up to the brim. He said to them, "Now draw some out, and take it to the chief steward." So they took it. When the steward tasted the water that had become wine, and did not know where it came from (though the servants who had drawn the water knew), the steward called the bridegroom and said to him, "Everyone serves the good wine first, and then the inferior wine after the guests have become drunk. But you have kept the good wine until now." Jesus did this, the first of his signs, in Cana of Galilee, and revealed his glory; and his disciples believed in him.

1 Corinthians 13—The Greatest of These Is Love

If I speak in the tongues of mortals and of angels, but do not have love, I am a noisy gong or a clanging cymbal. And if I have prophetic powers, and understand all mysteries and all knowledge, and if I have all faith, so as to remove mountains, but do not have love, I am nothing. If I give away all my possessions, and if I hand over my body so that I may boast, but do not have love, I gain nothing.

Love is patient; love is kind; love is not envious or boastful or arrogant or rude. It does not insist on its own way; it is not irritable or resentful; it does not rejoice in wrongdoing, but rejoices in the truth. It bears all things, believes all things, hopes all things, endures all things.

Love never ends. But as for prophecies, they will come to an end; as for tongues, they will cease; as for knowledge, it will come to an end. For we know only in part, and we prophesy only in part; but when the complete comes, the partial will come to an end. When I was a child, I spoke like a child, I thought like a child, I reasoned like a child; when I became an adult, I put an end to childish ways. For now we see in a mirror, dimly, but then we will see face to face. Now I know only in part; then I will know fully, even as I have been fully known. And now faith, hope, and love abide, these three; and the greatest of these is love.

2 Corinthians 5:14-17—In Christ We Are a New Creation

For the love of Christ urges us on, because we are convinced that one has died for all; therefore all have died. And he died for all, so that those who live might live no longer for themselves, but for him who died and was raised for them.

From now on, therefore, we regard no one from a human point of view, even though we once knew Christ from a human point of view, we know him no longer in that way. So if anyone is in Christ, there is a new creation: everything old has passed away; see, everything has become new!

Colossians 3:12-17—Clothe Yourselves with Love

As God's chosen ones, holy and beloved, clothe yourselves with compassion, kindness, humility, meekness, and patience. Bear with one another and, if anyone has a complaint against another, forgive each other; just as the Lord has forgiven you, so you also must forgive. Above all, clothe yourselves with love, which binds everything together in perfect harmony. And let the peace of Christ rule in your hearts, to which indeed you were called in the one body. And be thankful. Let the word of Christ dwell in you richly; teach and admonish one another in all wisdom; and with gratitude in your hearts sing psalms, hymns, and spiritual songs to God. And whatever you do, in word or deed, do everything in the name of the Lord Jesus, giving thanks to God the Father through him.

1 John 3:18-24—Love One Another

Little children, let us love, not in word or speech, but in truth and action. And by this we will know that we are from the truth and will reassure our hearts before him whenever our hearts condemn us; for God is greater than our hearts, and he knows everything. Beloved, if our hearts do not condemn us, we have boldness before God; and we receive from him whatever we ask, because we obey his commandments and do what pleases him.

And this is his commandment that we should believe in the name of his Son Jesus Christ and love one another, just as he has commanded us. All who obey his commandments abide in him, and he abides in them. And by this we know that he abides in us, by the Spirit that he has given us.

Revelation 19:1-9—Wedding Feast of the Lamb

After this I heard what seemed to be the loud voice of a great multitude in heaven, saying, "Hallelujah! Salvation and glory and power to our God, for his judgments are true and just; he has judged the great whore who corrupted the earth with her fornication, and he has avenged on her the blood of his servants." Once more they said, "Hallelujah! The smoke goes up from her forever and ever." And the twenty-four elders and the four living creatures fell down and worshiped God who is seated on the throne, saying, "Amen. Hallelujah!"

And from the throne came a voice saying, "Praise our God, all you his servants, and all who fear him, small and great." Then I heard what seemed to be the voice of a great multitude, like the sound of many waters and like the sound of mighty thunderpeals, crying out, "Hallelujah! For the Lord our God the Almighty reigns. Let us rejoice and exult and give him glory, for the marriage of the Lamb has come, and his bride has made herself ready; to her it has been granted to be clothed with fine linen, bright and pure"—for the fine linen is the righteous deeds of the saints.

And the angel said to me, "Write this: Blessed are those who are invited to the marriage supper of the Lamb." And he said to me, "These are true words of God."

Several Psalms (including 23, 33, 37, 103, 117, 121, 145, and 148) are also worthy of consideration and should be reviewed by the pastor and the couple for potential inclusion in the service.

While these references are certainly not all inclusive, they serve to provide a base for the pastor and the couple to consider. Early on in the planning process, the couple, in consultation with the pastor, should review several scriptural passages to understand their content and meaning and the wedding message that may evolve out of them.

ADDITIONAL READINGS

In addition to readings from Scripture, several passages from secular literature may also be appropriate for the wedding service and may be offered by the pastor, a member of the wedding party, a family member, or a friend.

The reading may be prefaced by a brief statement as to its potential meaning for the wedding couple, such as:

> Reader: *(Bride's Name)* and *(Groom's Name)*, I share with you on this joyous occasion a reading which I believe will bring added meaning to your relationship and inspiration to your lives. It is titled *(Title of Piece)*.

Numerous secular readings exist that are appropriate and can be meaningful for the wedding ceremony.

- Several of William Shakespeare's sonnets (18 and 116, in particular)
- Sonnet XLIII (from *Sonnets from the Portuguese*) by Elizabeth Barrett Browning
- *On Love*, by Thomas à Kempis (1379–1471)

- *Desiderata*, by Max Erhmann
- Portions of *The Hymn of the Universe*, by Teilhard de Chardin
- Several of Kahlil Gibran's works (especially: *On Children*, *On Love*, and *On Marriage*)
- *The Magic of Love*, by Madeleine L'Engle
- *The Art of a Good Marriage*, by Wilferd Arlan Peterson
- *Sonnet 17*, by Pablo Neruda
- Selections from *The Hungering Dark*, by Frederick Buechner

Additional readings of a contemporary nature may be located on a variety of wedding-oriented websites (e.g., todays-weddings. com, allseasonsweddings.com, weddings.about.com). Remember, a wedding service is first and foremost a worship experience. Inclusion of secular readings should be in addition to, rather than a replacement for, readings from Scripture. The authorship and sources of web-based readings are often unclear. Review all secular readings for appropriateness.

INTERCESSORY PRAYER

The Intercessory Prayer functions to seek God's blessing on the couple, the vows they make, and their future lives together. The prayer may be offered by the pastor, or may be a unison prayer voiced by the entire gathering.

Intercessory Prayer (option 1)

Eternal God, creator of all that lives,
we ask your blessing this day on
   (Bride's Name) and *(Groom's Name)*
   who come now to join in marriage.
Enable them to give their vows
   with a sense of honesty and integrity.
Enable them to grow deeper in love

and richer in peace
that they may share with the world
the blessings of your love;
through Jesus Christ our Lord. Amen.

Intercessory Prayer (option 2)

Gracious and caring God,
your generous love transcends all humanity.
As (Bride's Name) and (Groom's Name)
witness to their faith
and come seeking your blessing,
we ask that you fill them with peace and joy
in all their days together.
Guide them in their living
to seek your counsel and do your will
that their home may be a refuge,
a sanctuary of goodness.
Bless them with strength in need,
comfort in sorrow,
forgiveness in adversity, and
wisdom in their devotion to one another.
May their life together be filled with Christ's love,
keeping them faithful and true throughout their days,
through Christ Jesus our Lord. Amen.

Intercessory Prayer (option 3)

Lord God, source of all love,
pour out your Holy Spirit
on (Bride's Name) and (Groom's Name),
as they offer their lives to each other, and
grant that they may do so in grace and truth.
Grant that the covenant in which they are united
to one another
be a knitting of mind and soul, and
may they be examples to others
of your love and joy.

Fill them with patience, kindness, gentleness, and wisdom,
   that their lives will shine brightly in the darkness
   as they embark on a new journey,
   as new and exciting paths unfold before them.
Amen.

EXCHANGE OF VOWS

In the context of the vows to be exchanged, the couple declares publicly and legally their commitment to each other as husband and wife. The woman and man face each other, joining hands, and speak to their vows of marriage. The pastor should prompt the couple, line by line. Advise caution when couples suggest that they recite their vows without prompting. The stress typically present often results in one or the other (or both) participants completely forgetting what was thought to be securely memorized. If the couple insists on a solo recitation, however, the pastor should have a copy of the vows at hand to offer prompting when necessary. The exchange of vows typically begins with the pastor asking a question of intent, followed by the recital of vows by the bride and groom.

Question of Intent

Pastor: *(Bride's Name)* and *(Groom's Name)*,
   if it is your intention to be united
   in this holy bond and covenant of marriage,
   please signify that desire by facing each other
   and joining your right hands.

Vows (option 1)

I, *(Groom's Name)*, take you,
   (Bride's Name), to be my wife,
to have and to hold from this day forward,
   under all circumstances and at all times,

to be caring, faithful, honest, and loving to you,
until we are parted by death.

I, *(Bride's Name)*, take you,
   (Groom's Name), to be my husband,
to have and to hold from this day forward,
   under all circumstances and at all times,
      to be caring, faithful, honest, and loving to you,
      until we are parted by death.

Vows (option 2)

I, *(Bride's Name)*, take you,
   (Groom's Name), to be my husband.
In the presence of God, our families,
   and our friends as witnesses,
I give you my sacred vow that as your wife,
   I will support you, encourage you, comfort you,
      inspire you, grieve with you,
      and share with you our future together,
      so long as we both shall live.
I will respect you, trust you, and forgive you
   as we have been forgiven.
This is my solemn vow.

I, *(Groom's Name)*, take you,
   (Bride's Name), to be my wife.
In the presence of God, our families,
   and our friends as witnesses,
I give you my sacred vow that as your husband,
   I will support you, encourage you, comfort you,
      inspire you, grieve with you,
      and share with you our future together,
      so long as we both shall live.
I will respect you, trust you, and forgive you
   as we have been forgiven.
This is my solemn vow.

Vows (option 3)

Do you, (*Groom's Name*), take this woman
  whose hand you now hold,
to be your true and wedded wife;
    and do you solemnly promise before God
        and these witnesses,
    to love, honor, cherish, and protect her;
    to forsake all others and be faithful to her
        as long as you both shall live.
If so, please say, I do.
Groom: I do.

Do you, (*Bride's Name*), take this man
  who now holds your hand,
to be your true and wedded husband;
    and do you also solemnly promise before God
        and these witnesses
    to love, honor, cherish, and protect him;
    to forsake all others and be faithful to him
        as long as you both shall live.
If so, please say, I do.
Bride: I do.

Vows (option 4)

On this special day, and in the eyes of God,
I, (*Bride's Name*), take you, (*Groom's Name*),
  as my partner in life's journey.
I vow to encourage you through our walk together.
When the way becomes difficult or weary,
  I promise to stand by you, and with you,
  so that through our marriage,
      together we can accomplish all
      our hopes and dreams.

On this special day, and in the eyes of God,
I, (*Groom's Name*), take you, (*Bride's Name*),
  as my partner in life's journey.

I vow to encourage you through our walk together.
When the way becomes difficult or weary,
  I promise to stand by you, and with you,
    so that through our marriage,
      together we can accomplish all
      our hopes and dreams.

Vows (option 5)

(The following vows may be recited in unison.)
  As we stand beside the ocean tide,
    may our love always be as these
    never-ending waves that pour
    from beneath the depths of the sea;
  Your love came softly upon my heart,
    just as the foam comes softly
    from the ocean's flow,
    so there will never be a day
    without my love for you.
  I pledge myself to you this day.
  Our love will be as unchanging
    and dependable as the tide.
  As these waters nourish God's earth
    and sustain life,
      may my constant devotion
      nourish and sustain you
      until the end of time.

Vows (option 6)

(Bride's Name), because you came into my life I am
      no longer lonely.
  Because of you I sense that my life is new and refreshed.
  You are my love, my joy, my friend, my very being.
  I give myself to you freely and without reservation
    to be your faithful and loving husband
      so we may share our lives as long as God allows.

(Groom's Name), because you came into my life I am
no longer lonely.
Because of you I sense my life is new and refreshed.
You are my love, my joy, my friend, my very being.
I give myself to you freely and without reservation
to be your faithful and loving wife
so we may share our lives as long as God allows.

Vows for a Service of Renewal

(Wife's Name) and *(Husband's Name)*,
(number of years) years ago you embraced each other
in marriage,
taking each other for all that life should offer.
Do you desire to reaffirm those vows?
If so, please respond, I do.
I, *(Wife's Name)*, once again take you, *(Husband's Name)*,
as the love of my life.
I promise to laugh with you,
grow even deeper in love with you, grieve with you,
and offer to you my care, trust, and respect.
I am whole because of you.
(Husband's Name), you are my love.
I, *(Husband's Name)*, once again take you, *(Wife's Name)*,
as the love of my life.
I promise to laugh with you,
grow even deeper in love with you, grieve with you,
and offer to you my care, trust, and respect.
I am whole because of you.
(Wife's Name), you are my love.

BLESSING AND EXCHANGE OF RINGS

It is traditional that couples exchange wedding rings after they
exchange their vows. The exchanging of rings expresses the
couple's promise of fidelity and faithfulness to each other. The

wedding ring is an outward symbol or sign of an inward and spiritual bonding. Two hearts, two lives, two rings are united as one.

During the wedding ceremony, the rings are usually held by the best man until required for the exchange ritual. Some couples will ask that the rings be attached to a small pillow carried by the ring bearer. This can be a dangerous practice, however, in that there are times when the ribbon attaching the rings will become knotted, making it almost impossible to remove the rings with any sense of decorum. It is better to attach a decorative pair of rings to the pillow rather than risk such a dilemma.

Many married couples have indicated that the ring ceremony was the most memorable moment of the wedding service. It needs to be creative and meaningful. The traditional, "With this ring, I thee wed," while certainly appropriate and time-honored, is typically being replaced with more creative applications.

The pastor will generally request receiving the rings from the best man, after which a statement may be made as to their symbolism. This statement is followed by a prayer of blessing over the rings.

Blessing and Exchange of Rings (option 1)

Pastor: These rings are an outward, visible symbol of the covenant made this day, and signify the uniting of (*Bride's Name*) and (*Groom's Name*) in holy marriage. Let us pray:
Bless, O Lord, the giving and receiving of these rings, that they who wear them may share in your grace, dwell in your peace, and continue in your favor. Amen.

Groom: (*Bride's Name*), I give you this ring as a sign of my love and my faithfulness, in the name of the Father, and of the Son, and of the Holy Spirit. Amen.

Bride: (*Groom's Name*), I give you this ring as a sign of my love and my faithfulness, in the name of the Father, and of the Son, and of the Holy Spirit. Amen.

Blessing and Exchange of Rings (option 2)

Pastor: The ring is a symbol of the commitment which
binds these two together. The rings are made of
pure gold, to remind you to keep your love
pure. Their unbroken circle symbolizes your
unending love for one another. Wear them
with pride; wear them with integrity. Let us
pray:
Lord, we ask your blessing on these precious
rings. May the symbolism they carry hold true
for this couple. May these rings be reminders of
their love for one another and also of your love
for them—pure and unending. Amen.

Groom: *(Bride's Name)*, I give you this ring as I give you
myself, with love and affection, now and for all
time to come.

Bride: *(Groom's Name)*, I give you this ring as I give
you myself, with love and affection, now and
for all time to come.

Blessing and Exchange of Rings (option 3)

Pastor: These rings are an outward sign of an inward
bond; a spiritual bond that unites two hearts in
love and affection. It is a circle that has neither
beginning nor ending: a circle of precious gold
as a symbol of the richness of your devotion.
The rings you exchange signify to all your marriage to one another. Let us pray:
Lord God, in the golden glow of this day, we
ask your blessing on these rings that *(Bride's
Name)* and *(Groom's Name)* now exchange.
May they live together in peace and comfort; in
love and abiding joy. May these rings be worn
with a deep sense of faith, hope, and trust. We
pray this in Jesus' name. Amen.

Groom: *(Bride's Name)*, my love, I can think of no finer gift to give than this sacred symbol of my unending love for you. I hereby pledge my love, my loyalty, and my life to you. Please wear this ring as a sign of the love we share. In the name of the Father, and of the Son, and of the Holy Spirit. Amen.

Bride: *(Groom's Name)*, my love, I can think of no finer gift to give than this sacred symbol of my unending love for you. I hereby pledge my love, my loyalty, and my life to you. Please wear this ring as a sign of the love we share. In the name of the Father, and of the Son, and of the Holy Spirit. Amen.

Blessing and Exchange of Rings (option 4)

Pastor: Let these rings be given as symbols of unending love; the precious love that is shared by *(Bride's Name)* and *(Groom's Name)*.

Groom: *(Bride's Name)*, I give you this ring as a reminder of my love and my faithfulness for all time.

Bride: *(Groom's Name)*, I give you this ring as a reminder of my love and my faithfulness for all time.

Blessing and Exchange of Rings for a Renewal Service

Pastor: *(Bride's Name)* and *(Groom's Name)*, years ago you circled one another's fingers with bands of gold as a symbol of your never-ending love; as a sign of your willingness to live within God's circle of love.

Husband: *(Bride's Name)*, I again give you this ring to wear, honoring the vows that we make today. Wear it as a symbol of my continued love for you.

Wife: *(Groom's Name)*, I too give you this ring to wear, honoring the vows that we make today. Wear it as a symbol of my continued love for you.

UNITY CANDLE CEREMONY

A fairly recent addition to the wedding service, the unity candle ceremony is yet another sign that the husband and wife have become one.

If a unity candle is used in the service, the two side candles are lit first, often by the mothers of the wedding couple as they are escorted to their seats prior to the processional. An alternative would be to have the mothers or parents of the bride and groom light the side candles following the Presentation of the couple. The side candles are removed by the bride and groom during the unity candle liturgy and joined together to light the center candle. As the center candle is lit by the bride and groom, a reading may be offered to add to the drama.

Typically, the lighted candles of the wedding couple are then extinguished and placed back into their holders. An option for the wedding couple is to allow their individual candles to remain lighted and be returned to their respective holders. This action symbolizes that, although the two are joined and become one, as represented in the center candle, each person still is a unique individual, and the gift of God's light continues to shine in and through that individual. The three lit candles symbolize the celebration of the bride and groom as individuals and of their union in marriage.

If preferred, rather than a reading being offered during the candle lighting ceremony, there may be a time of silence so that the congregation can focus on the symbolic act taking place at the altar. A musical interlude is yet another option available during this liturgy.

Some couples choose to perform the mother's rose presentation at this point in the service, rather than following the Presentation.

Unity Candle (option 1)

(Side candles are extinguished after lighting the unity candle.)

(Bride's Name) and *(Groom's Name)*, you are two unique and individual people and the burning side candles represent your lives at this moment in time. To bring completeness and true satisfaction to your lives, there needs to be a merging of these two distinct flames into one. From this day forward your thoughts shall be for one another rather than for yourself. Your joys and sorrows will be shared as one; your hopes and dreams become united. As you each take a candle from the side and light the center, or unity, candle, you will merge your flames, then extinguish your individual candles and allow the unity candle to represent the union of your two lives. May the glowing radiance of this one light be a testimony to the love you share.

Unity Candle (option 2)

(Side candles remain lighted after lighting unity candle.)

(Bride's Name) and *(Groom's Name)* give of themselves in love, but they do not give their individuality away, for it was that individuality and uniqueness of character that first brought this couple together. A balanced and harmonious relationship is one in which neither person is absorbed by the other. The ultimate strength of a marriage, therefore, comes not from their melting into one but from the forging of two individuals to each other. As a symbol of that forging of human love by two unique souls, *(Bride's Name)* and *(Groom's Name)* allow their individual candles to remain lighted. These side candles remain burning to symbolize the continuing importance of each person's individual integrity within the context of marriage. By allowing the flame of the two smaller candles to remain lit, they also accept the individuality of each other as a means to the fulfillment of their oneness together. The larger, center candle symbolizes that together they can become more than either could alone.

Unity Candle (option 3—
a Reading based on Ruth 1:16-17)

(The following reading is offered as the wedding couple comes forward and lights the center unity candle. This passage is also appropriate for a couple who elects to light the unity candle as a part of renewing their vows.)

The ancient candle ceremony is a symbol of
    the one-flesh principle in marriage.
The two become one as if one
    were part of the flesh of the other.
The love that emerges from this unity is best described
    by Ruth's words to Naomi in the Old Testament:
"Do not press me to leave you
    or to turn back from following you!
Where you go, I will go;
    where you lodge, I will lodge;
your people shall be my people,
    and your God my God.
Where you die, I will die—
    there will I be buried.
May the LORD do thus and so to me,
    and more as well,
if even death parts me from you!"

Unity Candle Incorporating
Children of the Wedding Couple

With more and more couples embarking on second marriages, often with children from the previous marriage, it is meaningful to include them in the wedding service. This can easily be accomplished as a part of the unity candle service or in one of its alternatives. After lighting the unity candle, each parent may offer a dedication statement or similar commitment to the children from the spouse's previous marriage. Such an act is most meaningful and memorable when drafted as a letter, which can be printed out and given to the children.

Unity Candle with Children (option 1)

Dear *(Children's Names)*, I promise this day to love you as my own. I will love you unconditionally; without reservation; without expectation. I will care for you as my own and tend to your needs.

I promise you that I will do my best and will make every effort to offer sound guidance and direction. You can expect to hear words of kindness and inspiration from me each day. I will respect you and honor you and will be there for you in times of distress and discouragement, as well as in those times of joy and accomplishment.

With all my love, *(Bride's Name)* and *(Groom's Name)*.

Unity Candle with Children (option 2)

(From the Bride to the Groom's child. Can also be adapted for other situations.)
To *(Child's Name)*:

Two very special people came into my life a few years ago. From the very first time I met you, you have both had a very special place in my heart. Your beautiful smiles and great hugs just make me love you more and more every time we're together.

Your dad has made me so very happy and, as we begin our lives together as a new family, I hope that you will both be happy too. I love your dad a lot and I love you very much too.

I will always love you, and I will be there for you whenever you need me. I promise to try to be the best stepmom ever.

Thank you, *(Child's Name)* and *(Groom's Name)*, for loving me.

Unity Candle with Children (option 3)

(The pastor offers words of introduction, followed by words to the children of the wedding couple.)

To Parents: *(Bride's Name)* and *(Groom's Name)*, there are children who will share in this marriage. The blending of this newly created family will have a deep and lasting influence on their lives.

Surely it will both enrich and complicate their precious lives. But also please know that the children will have much to contribute to your marriage and to this new family. In order for your home to be happy and filled with peace, it is paramount that there be a generous measure of love offered and understanding given. (Bride's Name) and (Groom's Name), may the love you share likewise be shared with (Children's Names). May it be so.

To Children: (Children's Names), please know also that you are a vital part of this newly-created family and (Bride's Name) and (Groom's Name) vow to give you their unconditional love. No doubt, your lives will be touched by this marriage. And, not only will you have a share in this family but also a very important role. Your role will be to help, support, and encourage each other as you grow and mature into the very best that you can be. May it always be so.

ALTERNATIVES TO UNITY CANDLE

Several alternatives to the unity candle ritual are increasingly preferred by wedding couples. These include a hand ritual, water bath, and salt ritual. Examples of these rather unique and powerful ceremonies follow. For couples who are renewing their wedding vows, any of these rituals may be adapted to bring meaning to their service of reaffirmation.

Hand Ritual

The Hand Ritual is a very meaningful symbol of the joining of hands in marriage. The narrative may be read alternately by the best man and maid/matron of honor, as participation from the

47

wedding party adds immensely to the service. The words of this rather unique ritual speak to the care and love that each set of hands will display throughout the course of the marriage.

Hand Ritual

(The pastor offers words of introduction, then addresses the bride.)
(Bride's Name), take *(Groom's Name)*'s hands in yours and look at his palms.

These hands are now large and strong. Remember, too, that they were once very tiny hands; hands formed by God.

His mother and father held these hands and counted his fingers when he was born. They held on to those hands as he learned to walk.

Everyone who loves him held those hands and taught him to be the man he is today.

His family taught him to love and trust with those hands; to gently hold a new puppy or to touch the cheek of a new baby.

These hands reached out for support; to hold on to someone else when he might have been afraid of falling down or failing in some way.

These hands have grown in love; to share love; to be kind and gentle, yet strong and firm; to touch your cheek, to wipe away your tears, to hold your hands in love; for comfort, for strength, for hope.

These hands will hold your hands when your child is born. These hands will hold that child with gentleness and warmth.

These hands will hold your hands in illness to provide comfort and prayer.

These hands were first the hands of a son, now a husband, and perhaps someday of a father. These hands, formed by God, are indeed a gift to you. Treasure these hands; love these hands, as you grow old together.

Cherish your gift, today and every tomorrow.
(The pastor addresses the groom.)
Now, *(Groom's Name)*, I ask you to hold *(Bride's Name)*'s hands in yours. Look at her palms, so soft, smooth, and gentle. These hands fit so well in yours as you hold and caress them.

Like yours, her hands were not always what you hold today. Her hands, too, were much smaller. These hands wrapped around her father's finger as he looked at her in awe the day she was born. These hands held on tight, in trust, in faith, in love.

Her parents also held her hands as she learned to walk and stand on her own. These hands learned trust, but they also learned independence, when someone tried to show her how to do something and she said, "I can do it myself!" and most times, she did.

Her family likewise held these hands; a family who guided her to become the woman you fell in love with.

These hands will gently touch your cheek; will hold you when you feel down and out; will care for you when you're sick.

These hands will reach for you in the middle of the night, searching for warmth and comfort.

These hands, a daughter's hands, now the hands of a precious wife, a soul mate, and friend, may someday be the hands that belong to the mother of your children. These hands will hold your children and will nurture, guide, protect, and love them as no one else could.

Hold these dear hands in yours as the years pass by. Hold them tight. Hold them for a lifetime, knowing that her hands were also a gift from God. Treasure them with your whole being, today and for all your tomorrows.

Prayer following Recitation

(Offered by the pastor)
Gracious and loving God, bless these hands that you see before you this day. May they always be held by one another; held in love and faith. Give *(Bride's Name)* and *(Groom's Name)* the needed strength to hold firm during the storms of life and during any times of disillusionment.

Help these precious and loving hands continue building a relationship founded in your grace; a relationship rich in caring, devoted to one another, and always marked by your love. May *(Bride's Name)* and *(Groom's Name)* see their own hands and each other's as instruments of healing, protection, shelter, and guidance.

We ask this in the name of your Son, Jesus Christ. Amen.

Water Washing Ritual

In order to conduct a water washing ritual, two small pitchers of water need to be placed on the altar before the service. A large, empty bowl is placed between the two pitchers. At the appropriate time, the wedding couple is invited to pour water into the bowl as a symbol of two lives coming together. A brief introduction to the ceremony as well as a blessing is offered by the pastor.

Water Washing Ritual Introduction

(Bride's Name) and *(Groom's Name)*, on this solemn occasion, are joining their two lives into a mutual relationship based on God's precious gifts of faith, hope, and love. As a symbol of the newness of live that they now share, *(Bride's Name)* and *(Groom's Name)* pour water from their respective pitchers—their baptized beings, their lives—into a common vessel.

Water Washing Ritual Blessing

(The pastor asks the couple to join hands over the common vessel and offers a simple blessing prayer.)
Lord God,

   (Bride's Name) and *(Groom's Name)* stand before you and symbolically offer themselves to each other through this gift of life-giving water. Water cleanses, water refreshes, water heals, and water gives birth. We pray, Lord, that *(Bride's Name)* and *(Groom's Name)* may be cleansed, refreshed, healed, and experience a wonderful sense of new birth in this marriage.

Water Washing Ritual Pouring

(Following the prayer, the pastor places his or her hands in the common vessel and scoops out generous amounts of water, which is then

poured over the joined hands of the couple. The pouring should be performed three times; once each in the name of the Father, the Son, and the Holy Spirit.)

(Bride's Name) and (Groom's Name),
> your marriage be blessed,
> your lives cleansed, healed, and renewed,
in the name of the Father, and of the Son,
> and of the Holy Spirit. Amen.

(A small towel is then draped over the couples' hands. The groom gently pats both sets of hands dry—first the bride's and then his own. The pastor then extends a hand to receive the towel.)

Sand Ritual

The blending of grains of sand is increasingly being employed in the wedding service as a contemporary alternative to the more traditional unity candle liturgy. The sand ceremony, as an alternative to the lighting of the unity candle, is also quite appropriate for an outdoor or seaside setting.

In this ceremony the bride and groom each take a small, clear container filled with sand and pour it into a larger, clear vessel, such as a vase or bowl.

Sand Ritual Introduction

The sand ceremony symbolizes the union of "two into one." (Bride's Name) and (Groom's Name) will combine the sand they each bring to this wedding service into a common vessel, which symbolizes their new life together as one. Husband and wife come together as family, not only in the union of bride and groom but also in the blending of families and friends. Their different sands represent everything that (Bride's Name) and (Groom's Name) have been in the past or will become in the future. The individual sands, once poured into the unity vessel, can never be separated; they are forever blended, just as the lives of (Bride's Name) and (Groom's Name) are now forever blended together as one.

Sand Ritual Prayer

Lord God, just as *(Bride's Name)* and *(Groom's Name)* have blended these sands, may their lives and their love be forever blended. Just as these grains of sand can no longer be separated and returned to their individual containers, so may the family bond be unbreakable. Amen.

Sand Ritual: Incorporating Loved Ones

Children by a previous marriage or other immediate family members (parents, brothers, sisters) can be dramatically incorporated into the sand ritual. Each person brings a small container of different-colored sand to the altar. Along with the wedding couple, the wedding party, children by a previous marriage, and other family members may be invited to blend their different sands in the common, clear vessel.

Sand Ritual Introduction

Truly, we are all members of one family, God's family. Today as *(Bride's Name)* and *(Groom's Name)* seal their marriage vows with the exchange of rings, they also make a commitment to their greater families. *(Names of Persons Participating in Ritual)* each play an important and dynamic role in this marriage and they now join *(Bride's Name)* and *(Groom's Name)* in this commitment by contributing a part of themselves to this new entity.

The relationship created today is symbolized through the pouring of the sands of self into a common vessel, or family.

Please pour your sand of self into this common vessel to symbolize the joining of your lives.

As these grains of sand come together in a colorful blending (pastor to stir and blend the different-colored sands at this point), so too are your many and different lives now and forever blended as one.

Prayer

Holy God, creator of the immeasurable sands of the earth,
send your blessing of love and unity upon this family.

May their love abide in one another and may their lives
   dwell within your heart.
We pray this in Jesus' name. Amen.

Salt Ritual

Salt is known as both a preservative and an enhancer of flavors.
Salt was truly a valued commodity in ancient days. It served as a
symbol of the nature of the covenant God made with the Levites
(see Numbers 18:19). A Covenant of Salt represents a binding
contract, never to be broken. It is meant to endure forever.

Scripture records that when a contract was made, each party
placed a pinch of salt into the pocket of the other party. It was
implied that if every grain of salt could be sorted, identified, and
returned to the rightful owner, the contract could be broken. The
salt ritual is popular with many couples and may be used in place
of the sand ceremony.

In terms of the wedding service, the bride and groom each
carry a small bag or cloth packet with a drawstring or other means
of enclosure. A small amount of salt (one or two tablespoons) is
placed in the packet prior to the service. During the wedding, the
pastor may offer the following introduction to the ritual and,
upon completion of the exchange, extend a blessing prayer.

Salt Ritual Introduction

Salt was a very precious commodity in ancient days. In the
Bible it symbolized the sealing of a covenant and indicated a
binding, irrevocable contract. When a contract was made, each
party put a pinch of salt into the pocket of the other person. It
was said that if ever each grain of salt could be sorted, identified, and returned to its rightful owner, the contract could be
broken.

(Bride's Name) and (Groom's Name), I ask you now to take out
your packets and remove a pinch of salt from each. Now, place
your pinch of salt in the other's packet. Your lives, like the salt
you have just exchanged, have become blended into one. The

exchange you have just made is representative of the sealing of your covenant—a covenant never to be broken.

Salt Ritual Prayer

Let us pray:
O God, (Bride's Name) and (Groom's Name) have acted
   to seal with salt the wedding covenant
     they make this day.
May the intermingling of these grains never be sorted,
   never be identified as one person's or the other's.
As the grains of salt have come together to form one,
   so too (Bride's Name) and (Groom's Name)
     have become one.
Bless this their covenant and allow them to be
   the "salt of the earth" for one another and for you.
In Jesus' name we pray. Amen.

Glass Breaking Ritual

While typically an important element in a Jewish wedding, the powerful symbolism of the breaking of a glass is certainly appropriate in a Christian setting as well. There are numerous interpretations offered for this unique experience: the destruction of the temple in Jerusalem; that life brings sadness as well as joy; the symbolic breaking of the hymen; although the couple comes together in a single union, the world is broken and needs mending; the couple's happiness (or children) will be as plentiful as the shards of glass.

The glass must be wrapped in a small towel or other appropriate protective material that will prevent the broken glass from flying. When the pastor completes the introduction to the ritual, the groom places the glass (in its protective cover) on the floor and stomps on it. In a Jewish service the groom would shout, *Mazel Tov* (an expression of good luck). In a Christian wedding the groom might say, "May our marriage never break!"

Glass Breaking Ritual Introduction

(A pastor may introduce the ritual by offering words such as these.)

(Bride's Name) and (Groom's Name) have chosen to include a rather unusual ritual within their wedding service today. The breaking of a glass is a typical element in a Jewish wedding, yet there is a richness of symbolism in this act that is meaningful for all God's children. The glass symbolizes the fact that love and relationships are truly fragile, and must be cared for and not broken. The breaking of the glass is a reminder that sometimes a single thoughtless act, a breach of trust, or an act of infidelity can damage a marriage in ways that are truly difficult to undo; just as it would be extremely difficult to undo the breaking of this glass. May any barriers that presently exist in your lives be broken and shattered like this glass. It is our hope and prayer for you today, (Bride's Name) and (Groom's Name), that your love for one another will remain until the many pieces of this glass come together again.

DECLARATION OF MARRIAGE

The Declaration of Marriage takes place following the vows and exchange of rings and other ceremonial components of the wedding service. The Declaration is the religious and legal announcement of the couple's marriage.

Declaration (option 1)

(Bride's Name) and (Groom's Name)
   have made this covenant of marriage
   before God and this congregation, and so,
I announce to you that they are husband and wife,
   in the name of the Father, the Son,
     and the Holy Spirit.
Those whom God has joined together,
   let no one divide. Amen.

Declaration (option 2)

(*Bride's Name*) and (*Groom's Name*),
   you have made your promises to each other,
   to be faithful and true in your life together,
Because you have pledged your love in this fashion,
   I announce to all that you are husband and wife,
In the name of the Father, the Son,
   and the Holy Spirit. Amen.

Declaration (option 3)

Now that (*Bride's Name*) and (*Groom's Name*)
   have given themselves to each other
   by sharing solemn vows,
     with the joining of hands,
     and the offering and receiving of rings,
I declare them to be husband and wife.
In the name of the Father, the Son,
   and the Holy Spirit. Amen.

Declaration for a Renewal Service

Before God and this gathering
   (*Bride's Name*) and (*Groom's Name*)
   have renewed their precious wedding vows.
They have reaffirmed the covenant of marriage and so I
   declare them to be renewed as husband and wife,
In the name of God the Father, the Son,
   and the Holy Spirit.

(*Following the Declaration of Marriage, the pastor typically invites the groom to greet the bride with a kiss.*)

BLESSING OF THE MARRIAGE

Numerous prayers for the blessing of the marriage are available, both in denominational resources and in secular literature.

Blessing prayers should certainly speak to the importance of the event as well as offer God's grace for the future. During the blessing prayer, the couple may either remain standing or kneel as the pastor prays. At the conclusion of the Blessing Prayer, the pastor may invite the gathered congregation to recite the Lord's Prayer.

Couples may request the reading of "The Apache Blessing Prayer" or "The Traditional Irish Blessing" as an alternative blessing prayer. Appropriate versions of either prayer can be found on the Internet.

Blessing (option 1)

Gracious and loving God,
we thank you for the love that you share with
   (Bride's Name) and (Groom's Name).
Thank you for reminding us that
     in the covenant of marriage
   there is a gift of spiritual unity
     not only between this couple
   but also between Christ Jesus and his holy Church.
Send your blessing upon
   (Bride's Name) and (Groom's Name),
   that they may truly keep their marriage covenant,
     love and honor each other,
   cherish each other in wisdom and godliness;
   and may their home be a place of sacred sanctuary.
May God bless you and keep you
   for all your days to come. Amen.

Blessing (option 2)

Spirit of love, in all your dimensions, may (Bride's Name) and (Groom's Name) know and experience great love together and may their lives be reflective of the wondrous joy they share. May they strengthen one another in sorrow and times of despair, and be found as faithful, loving companions. May their love be strong and radiant, shining brightly on those around them. May their home be a haven of love, peace, and joy, and may your presence journey with them, now and forever. Amen.

Blessing (option 3)

Lord, our God,
we thank you for this joyous day and the celebration
  of love we share in.
May *(Bride's Name)* and *(Groom's Name)* find that
  their love flourishes each day,
  growing stronger, deeper,
  and more meaningful as time passes.
Bless them with the precious gifts of trust, compassion,
  forgiveness, and truth that they may
    nurture one another
  and grow together in love, peace, and joy. Amen.

Blessing (option 4—
Prayer of Saint Francis of Assisi, adapted)

Lord, make us instruments of your peace;
where there is hatred, let us sow love;
where there is injury, pardon;
where there is discord, union;
where there is doubt, faith;
where there is despair, hope;
where there is darkness, light;
and where there is sadness, joy;
O Divine Master,
grant that we may not so much seek
to be consoled as to console;
to be understood as to understand,
to be loved as to love.
For it is in giving that we are pardoned,
and it is in dying that we are born to eternal life.
Amen.

(Following the Blessing Prayer, it is appropriate to include the Lord's Prayer.)

The Lord's Prayer (traditional— other versions may be used)

Our Father, who art in heaven,
  hallowed be thy name.
Thy kingdom come,
  thy will be done on earth as it is in heaven.
Give us this day our daily bread.
And forgive us our trespasses,
  as we forgive those who trespass against us.
And lead us not into temptation,
  but deliver us from evil.
For thine is the kingdom, and the power,
  and the glory, forever.
Amen.

DISMISSAL WITH BLESSING

During the Dismissal with Blessing, the pastor offers a concluding prayer of blessing for the couple and the congregation present. Following the prayer the pastor introduces the newly-married couple to those present.

Dismissal (option 1)

May this day shine throughout your lives
  and may you ever care for one another.
May the grace of God be with you always
  and may your lives be filled with Christ's presence.
May God's Holy Spirit watch over you,
  guide you, and nurture you.
Go forth in God's love,
  be a blessing to one another and to God.
Amen.

Dismissal (option 2)

The grace of God attend to your every need,
the love of Christ surround and comfort you,
the presence of the Holy Spirit allow you to
live in faith, share in hope,
experience great joy, and grow in love. Amen.

Dismissal (option 3)

God the Father, Son, and Holy Spirit
shine upon you, be gracious to you,
look upon you with gentle kindness,
and fill your hearts with peace.
Amen.

INTRODUCTION OF COUPLE

After inviting the couple to greet each other with the traditional kiss, the pastor introduces the couple. The manner of introduction should be discussed with the couple during the completion of an information form. This information is necessary, as many brides today are opting to retain their maiden names or otherwise desire to be introduced with the use of their first name.

Introduction (option 1)

Family and friends, it is indeed my pleasure to introduce to you Mr. and Mrs. *(Groom's Full Name)*.

Introduction (option 2)

Ladies and gentlemen, I have the pleasure of introducing to you (for the first time), Mr. and Mrs. *(Groom's First Name)* and *(Bride's First Name)* *(Last Name)*.

Introduction (option 3)

I introduce to you, as husband and wife, *(Groom's Full Name)* and *(Bride's Full Name)*.

Introduction for a Renewal Service

Let us now greet *(Wife's Name)* and *(Husband's Name)*, who have renewed their commitment to love and care for one another. *(It would certainly be appropriate at this time for the pastor to invite applause, if others have not done so already.)*

RECESSIONAL

The recessional is essentially the processional in reverse order, except that the ushers always escort the bridesmaids down the aisle as they leave the sanctuary. After the bridal party exits, it is appropriate for the pastor to approach the first row of pews on the bride's side and gesture that the family may exit. The pastor then moves to the groom's side and does the same. This is then followed by the pastor alternating sides and dismissing the gathered congregation.

CHAPTER THREE

WEDDING
MEDITATIONS

W hile sermons or meditations are not included in every wedding service, pastors will sometimes receive positive response to the question of inclusion of a wedding homily. Sermon lengths vary, and are typically guided by the style, format, and context of the wedding service. Pastors should, in all cases, offer the inclusion of a brief message as the wedding is, first and foremost, a service of worship.

In most every instance the wedding sermon or meditation should draw on the theme of the other liturgical elements (vows, blessings, and prayers) selected. Likewise, it is proper and advantageous to offer some amount of reflection on the wedding couple's lives. A note of familiarity with the wedding couple provides for a greater sense of hospitality and witness to the gathered community.

While the ultimate success of the wedding service does not rest on the sermon, a sermon is a unique opportunity for the pastor to provide insight into the meaning of the event for the couple, as well as for the gathered community of family and friends. In essence, the sermon provides for sharing witness to the love of Jesus Christ and the love of God's creation, especially the wedding couple.

LOVE IS IN THE AIR

(Based on 1 Corinthians 1:1-13)

We are gathered on this beautiful spring day to witness the joining together of these two people; *(Bride's Name)* and *(Groom's Name)*, whose hearts and spirits are surely entwined as one. It is their stated desire to profess before God and this gathering their noble intention to journey through life together in a covenantal relationship. The love and affection that motivates these two people are expressed in so many wonderful ways.

We hear the word *love* used so often today, and it has so many different meanings to so many different people. True love, the love that I have seen in the eyes, the voices, and the hearts of *(Bride's Name)* and *(Groom's Name)*, is surely God's precious gift of romantic love. Their own love, so powerful and meaningful, is evident in the air this afternoon. No doubt it is also being felt by all of us as love is such a warm and contagious blessing.

True love is more than just a feeling or an emotion that changes with the seasons or moves with the mood of one person or the other. Love is a true commitment; it is a commitment that is meant to last a lifetime. Love is a sacrifice of oneself for the other, a giving totally one to the other.

There are those people who will say to me that "marriage is a 50/50 proposition." Nothing, however, I believe, could be further from the truth. Marriage is essentially a 100 percent giving of oneself to the other person; giving without reservation, giving without expectation, giving without seeking a return on one's investment so to speak. Paul's First Letter to the Corinthians reminds us all that "Love is patient; love is kind; love is not envious or boastful or arrogant or rude. It does not insist on its own way; it is not irritable or resentful; it does not rejoice in wrongdoing, but rejoices in the truth. It bears all things, believes all things, hopes all things, endures all things" (1 Corinthians 13:4-7).

And so, dear *(Bride's Name)* and *(Groom's Name)*, it is our charge to you on this your wedding day, to remember these powerful words. Be patient and kind. Never insist on your own way, but rather share in your hopes and dreams and ambitions. Arrogance and rudeness are two human characteristics which, left unbridled, can ruin lives; and I urge you to avoid them at all costs. Rejoice in the truth and you will come to know one another in so many beautiful and different ways. As your love grows and matures even more fully, you will truly discover that the deep and profound love that you share will help you bear any difficulties which may arise along your journey and you will, in your sharing of love's treasures, be quite capable of enduring most any obstacle that may confront you. Love which is real, honest, and forthright, as the Scriptures tell us, never fails. But be reminded that it takes commitment; it takes work; it takes large doses of forgiveness. If you make God the centerpiece or focus of your marriage, you will undoubtedly be able to overcome all diversity and divisiveness.

Your love for each other, in many ways, symbolizes the intense and genuine love that Christ Jesus has for his church—it is unwavering and it lasts forever. Today *(Bride's Name)* and *(Groom's Name)*, you make that same covenant of love in vowing to always be faithful to each other and to Christ your Savior. May it be so, now and forever. Amen.

A JOYOUS FESTIVAL AND CELEBRATION

(Bride's Name) and *(Groom's Name)*, you have freely come to this place, on this wonderful day, to offer yourselves to one another in the sacred act of marriage. Surely there are ties, no commitments, no bonds on this earth that are sweeter and more solemn than those you are about to make. This day that we gather to experience the gift of love that God has shared with you both, we are reminded that this wedding is both a sacred ceremony

and a joyous festival and celebration. While God has shared this wonderful gift of romantic love with the two of you, please be reminded that God, if given the opportunity, will also allow your love to grow and blossom in many more fruitful and enjoyable ways.

The marriage of heart, mind and body between a man and a woman is intended by God for your mutual joy and satisfaction. It is certainly meant to last a lifetime. It is expected to grow and flower into a relationship that reflects the image of Jesus Christ and his profound love for the church. And so, marriage is not to be entered into lightly. Rather, a couple must respond reverently and deliberately, and in accordance with the purposes for which marriage was instituted by God.

I am so delighted that you have chosen to exchange your vows today in this church, this house of worship. You make your vows before God and this congregation because you realize that God is so much a part of your lives and will be a part of your marriage. All that you are required to do is to extend that invitation; ask God to journey with you; ask God to guide you and inspire you; ask God to provide for your needs. Root your marriage and your lives in God's promise to be with you.

Allow your marriage to bring you closer and more in tune with one another. As you live, work, pray, and worship God together, you will discover that you are able to bear one another's burdens and share in one another's sorrows and joys; failures and accomplishments, defeats and good fortunes. Luke 1:37 reminds us: "For nothing will be impossible with God."

(*Bride's Name*) and (*Groom's Name*), cherish the relationship; cherish the love; cherish the commitment that you are establishing this day. Know deep down in your hearts that all things are possible with God as a part of your lives, a part of your marriage. May God bless you and keep you in the shadow of his wings of love. And may your lives be filled with faith, hope, and love— now and forever. Amen.

A CHRISTMAS WEDDING

We are deeply moved when we witness the beauty and joy of the Christmas story told so poignantly in carols and words and in meaningful images; the moving story of God's precious gift of his Son, Jesus Christ. Entering marriage in the height of the Christmas season also offers a gift of very special meaning to our service today. *(Bride's Name)* and *(Groom's Name)* have chosen to exchange their wedding vows not only in this church but also in the presence of the nativity display. The crèche or nativity display is a vivid reminder of the love of God shared with all humanity. From a stable scene in Bethlehem comes God's precious and enduring love incarnate; a gift to be opened for one and all to share.

The love of husband and wife likewise is a gift from God and this warm and tender love mirrors God's love for us. Today, in a very special way, it mirrors the love between *(Bride's Name)* and *(Groom's Name)*. We see God's joy in their faces; in those gleaming smiles we behold the presence of Christ Jesus, the One who came to love us and share with us a peace and contentment beyond all knowledge and understanding. With Christ Jesus in our lives, in our marriages, we become the recipients of a very special blessing of unity. In this gift we are drawn closer and closer to one another and to our Lord.

In Scripture, we hear of a spiritual unity that exists between Christ and his bride, the church. In these precious words, we learn of the unfathomable love of Christ for all humanity. Yes, dear family and friends, on this night, like the Christmas night in Bethlehem, God seeks to share a wonderful gift of love. And the night is silent; the night is holy. It is silent because our hearts are open to the voice of God reaching out with a very special word for all creation. It is holy because we celebrate not only the unity of Christ and his church, but also the special gift of unity that comes in the form of this marriage.

(Bride's Name) and *(Groom's Name)*, our prayer this day is that you both look upon your marriage as a very special Christmas gift

from God; a gift to be shared with each other; a gift to be shared with family and friends and loved ones; a gift to be shared in community with the church of Jesus Christ. May your marriage be filled with unity, harmony, respect, and a deep and abiding sense of love.

THE MUSIC OF LOVE

For a Stepson with a Love of Music

To *(Bride's Name)* and *(Groom's Name)*,

You have both been a part of my life now for some time and I wanted to share this letter with you today as you become husband and wife. *(Groom's Name)*, when your mother and I married, you and your siblings also became an important part of my life. There were many fun times together, and many of our family gatherings seemed to focus on your gift of music. Drum lessons, marching band, and so much more.

Just recently, I was awestruck when I heard you and *(Bride's Name)* sitting at the piano playing a duet. I was moved to look at you both as you sat there and made such beautiful music together—in so many ways. As I listened I was reminded of God's gift of love and the music that flows from this precious gift. The look of love in the eyes of both of you was simply amazing. The sound of your music was truly inspiring.

You and *(Bride's Name)* played on while your mom and I sat, watched, and listened. As you snuggled close together, there was a warmth and vibrancy that filled the air. My mind filled with thoughts of the love you two must be sharing. I watched four hands move ever-so-gracefully across the keyboard, sometimes separate, sometimes they seemed to cross, sometimes a gentle yet loving touch was witnessed.

The music varied from soft, hushed notes to loud, pulsating rhythms. Notes came swiftly and notes came slowly, seemingly at the same time. I experienced melody and harmony from a single composition. Yet, from time to time, a bit of disharmony was heard as you moved at a different pace or in opposition to each other.

I thought about those musical notes displayed on the page—moving up and down, sometimes close, sometimes more distant. As I heard you play, I was also moved to listen to the silence that occurred between the notes, knowing how these brief silences are so very important to the overall composition. I quickly began to realize that your lives together will very much be like the music you were playing.

(Bride's Name) and (Groom's Name), may the music of your lives together be as joyous and wonderful as the music you shared that day. Realize, however, that not unlike that musical composition you were playing, your lives will be filled with harmony, yet it is inevitable that brief periods of disharmony will chime forth. The rhythm of your lives may, at times, move slowly and steadily and at other times the notes will seem to be moving at a rapidly accelerating pace. Silent spaces may at times be evident and, I tell you today, that is okay. Loud and soft, slow and fast, up and down the scale, it all makes for one wonderful composition.

From ancient to modern, classical to rock, sacred to secular, each piece of music has a composer and I suggest to you both today that God is the one composing the music of your lives. Allow God to be the maestro of the music, listen to the rhythms of life, listen to the silences between the notes, strive for harmony together and the melody of your marriage will be one of genuine truth and absolute beauty.

(Bride's Name) and (Groom's Name), may the beat go on—forever and ever! Amen.

THE GENESIS OF MARRIAGE

"In the beginning," we are told, "when God created the heavens and the earth, the earth was a formless void and darkness covered the face of the deep, while a wind from God swept over the face of the waters" (Genesis 1:1). Later, in the book of

Genesis (2:7), we are reminded that, "then the LORD God formed man from the dust of the ground, and breathed into his nostrils the breath of life; and the man became a living being." In verse 18 God remarks, "It is not good that the man should be alone; I will make him a helper as his partner."

Then God sent the man to a deep sleep and God removed one of the man's ribs and used it to form the woman. So here in this creation account, we have God establishing the home, and it is for the establishment of a home that we all gather together on this day.

It seems to me that God had three basic purposes in creating man and woman and in establishing the marriage relationship. First, the creation of man, woman, and the marriage relationship allows for the reproduction and continuation of the human species. A second purpose is to foster deep feelings of love and affection between husband and wife. And third, God established the marriage covenant to satisfy human sexual desires and to make these desires honorable and virtuous. And so, as Genesis 1:31 proclaims, "God saw everything he had made, and indeed, it was very good"!

For these reasons, the marriage relationship—and the covenant that goes with it—is truly honorable and righteous in that it has been created by God. It is meant to be a lifelong covenant; a covenant which is binding, lasting, and to be experienced and truly enjoyed for the rest of your precious lives.

(Bride's Name) and *(Groom's Name)*, it is truly a joy and blessing that each of us has been invited to be a part of this very special day in your lives. Today, *(date)*, is the day that you become husband and wife. Today is that wonderful day that you establish your home together and begin a family of your own. Today is that day in which you stand before God and these people—family, friends, and loved ones—and enter into a lifelong, binding covenant. Truly, God smiles down upon you.

As you enter into this whole new arena of two lives joining together, I need to remind you that life will certainly have its ups and downs; that life, at times, may seem like it is throwing you a curve; that you are journeying through dark and fearful times. These are the times when you will truly need to look toward God

70

for strength, inspiration, and hope. But not only God, you need to be able to look to each other for those same blessings. As you grow and mature more fully, and place your faith—your very lives—in God's divine hands, you will see so clearly that you can and will trust in one another, that you will be able to encounter the difficulties of life together, and you will experience love growing stronger, firmer, and more reliable day-by-day. Allow God to be the centerpiece of your marriage and your lives and you will find a sense of contentment and peace beyond measure. *(Bride's Name)* and *(Groom's Name)*, laugh together, cry together, love together, share together, and care together. These are what make life together so livable for each and every one of us.

May the God of all creation, in the days and years ahead, see what God has made and joined together on this important occasion, and say "it is good—so very good!" May God bless your marriage covenant and fill you both with peace and joy.

To Blossom in Marriage

It was in a peaceful, divine garden that God brought man and woman to life. It was also in this garden setting that home and family and human relationships were born. Scripture, as we heard read earlier, tells us that God planted a garden in Eden and that in this garden God placed all kinds of trees and plants; this is a garden to be enjoyed and revered by all of God's creation.

What a joy and privilege it is for all of us as we share this day and witness the joining in marriage of *(Bride's Name)* and *(Groom's Name)*. Today, my friends, the divine seed has been planted for this couple to grow together as husband and wife and to fully blossom as the vibrant and precious flower that God has intended for marriage. What a beautiful metaphor for marriage, this image of a garden growing with the complete fullness of God's grace and blessings.

Yes, the seed has been planted today, but for quite some time now the soil in which this garden grows was being prepared. It has been carefully worked to provide the appropriate growing medium as *(Bride's Name)* and *(Groom's Name)* first met, became friends, developed a relationship, grew in love, and made their plans for this special day. Any garden, as we know, needs good soil with the proper texture, soil that is given proper nutrients and moisture, soil that has had the weeds and other barriers to good growth removed. *(Bride's Name)* and *(Groom's Name)* have very carefully and meticulously prepared the soil, the seedbed of their marriage.

In their growing together *(Bride's Name)* and *(Groom's Name)* have learned more and more of each other; nurtured that which is good; and, hopefully, removed the rocks, weeds, briars, and other impediments to a good foundational beginning. You will discover that your being together in harmony will add to the soil and its qualities for new and improved growth and development. Good soil allows for the growth of strong, firmly planted roots which, in turn, promote strong, healthy growth. The strong, abundant growth that you dedicate to your marriage in its formative years will then result in your marriage garden being a paradise.

As you journey together through life, know also that you will need to constantly maintain this garden of your love to keep it healthy and strong. Nurture it, refresh it from time to time, and feed it with love, patience, sincerity, forgiveness, and thoughtfulness, and you will experience it blooming and flowering in a multitude of ways. Your home and your lives will be like a garden in which you will reap a joyous and wonderful harvest; you will enjoy the fruits of your labor; and there will be an abundance of love that will enable others to also be nourished and fed.

So, dear *(Bride's Name)* and *(Groom's Name)*, I call you to take this image of the garden for your marriage and let it be a blessing to you and to those with whom you share your love.

TO A WELL KNOWN YOUNG COUPLE

(Bride's Name) and *(Groom's Name)*, it is truly a joy and honor for me to stand with you both on this your wedding day. It seems

that, through the grace of God, our lives have been entwined for a number of years. I remember way back when I first began to serve this church and saw you both among the children who would gather here at the altar for a children's message each Sunday morning. Time passed by and there you were, lifting your voices in praise as members of our children's choir. Later still, I would find you here for meetings of our youth group and Sunday school classes. You have both grown up here in this church, much as I have grown here also.

I can't help but think of the day you were baptized—prior to my arrival. No doubt, on that occasion, your parents vowed to raise you in the Christian faith and the congregation shared in that vow to assist in helping you embark on, explore, and nurture your faith journey. Your parents, grandparents, and this congregation have, in my view, succeeded immensely. This church and its greater church family have been a vital part of both your lives. We all certainly rejoice with you this day.

(Bride's Name) and (Groom's Name), I remind you that your journey in faith and life continues and today, on this solemn occasion, you simply embark in a new direction as traveling companions. It is our hope and prayer that you will continue to allow the light of Jesus Christ shine upon you, offering you light and wisdom to travel by. We pray that you will follow God's divine road map as contained in Scripture as your guide. Together, you will experience many days of smooth and uninterrupted travel, but that is not to expect that the journey will not be without its rough spots, detours, and speed bumps. When times get tough and the road seems so rough, when the raging torrents of life seem to be pouring down upon you, look to God and allow your love for one another and God's love for you both to be the cleansing and renewing force that grows and revitalizes your love and affection.

Not long ago I came upon a reading that defines *The Keys to Love* and I'd like to share these powerful words with you today. (*Read "The Keys to Love" by Robert M. Millay, available on the Internet, or choose another reading appropriate for the couple.*)

(Bride's Name) and (Groom's Name), may you learn from these simple yet heartfelt words and may you hold the vows you exchange today in the highest esteem. Know that your love for one another will grow as you apply these keys to your marriage and your journey in faith.

May God bless you and keep you, now and forever.

A DAUGHTER AND HER HUSBAND

(*Bride's Name*), my daughter and (*Groom's Name*), her husband to be, today you set sail on a new and beautiful course on the adventurous seas of life. How proud your mother and I are of what you both have accomplished in the years that you have known one another. We have seen your love for each other grow in so many wonderful ways. We have witnessed the glowing sparkle in your eyes, the poetry of love in your voices, and the caring and sharing that have become so important to you in your journey.

Together, hand-in-hand, you will travel familiar seas, safe and secure in the comfort of having had the course already charted out by others who have sailed on the seas of marriage before you. At other times in your life you will be faced with the need or desire to travel uncharted oceans, so to speak, waters that may seem to sweep you away into the torrents and raging currents of the world around you.

Leonard Sweet uses such a sailing metaphor in his "navigational text," *AquaChurch*. He talks about orienting by the North Star—Jesus the Christ, and studying your compass—the Bible. I remind you both, and all of us gathered here with you this day, that these are two of the most valuable resources you have for living out your journey. With Christ Jesus in your lives as a bright, shining star to light the way, and the Word of God found in Scripture as your map and compass, you will certainly be uniquely qualified to sail on calm and stormy seas and to greatly cherish your time together. With your deep and abiding faith and hope in Christ, know that the Lord our God, in times of stormy seas and turbulent tides, seeks to "lead you to still waters."

(Bride's Name) and *(Groom's Name)* have asked that I share a brief reading they came across recently by an unknown author. It is titled, *The Love You Have Will Change*, and it reminds us that we must go with the flow of the tides in order to preserve and maintain our relationships. *(Use this reading, available at vowson line.com, or choose another appropriate for the couple.)*

I think those words speak of our need to not only maintain the good, solid foundations that we have created but also to move with the changing tides that each of us face in our daily lives. We are like the dancers who, while perhaps barely touching, are partners in the same pattern of life, and love. We need to move with the tides, the ebb and flow of life, in order to experience growth, freedom, and a delightful sense of relationship.

So, dear *(Bride's Name)* and *(Groom's Name)*, if you'll pardon the pun, I wish you both *Bon Voyage* as you set sail on the seas of married life. May God bless you and keep you safe. May God watch over you in the calm and restful times, as well as in the moments of crises and darkness that will make up your lives. May God fill your sails with the often gentle, yet sometimes thrusting winds of the Spirit. And may you both be filled with the treasures of God's abundant blessings. Amen.

ONCE UPON A TIME

Once upon a time . . . life was good. Two young people met and fell madly in love. They were married . . . they raised a family and . . . they lived happily ever after. Fairy tales seem always to begin with "once upon a time" and end with the words "they lived happily ever after."

For you *(Bride's Name)* and *(Groom's Name)*, life as husband and wife comes with a caution (as it does for all couples): those who are married live happily ever after if they persevere in the task of loving each other and work diligently in creating a more loving and lasting relationship. Nothing in life comes easy, at least nothing that is truly honorable and worthwhile. Your marriage will take work, determination, and, at times, what seems to be a supreme amount of effort. You will need to daily build on your relationship to see it grow and mature into a truly satisfying life-long experience where joy and happiness outweigh the problems, the demands, the issues that will arise.

Love, I remind you, makes us whole and complete. And the love we share is stronger than any form of conflict, bigger than life's often-unexpected changes and demands, and deeper than the deepest fracture that seeks to divide. The love the two of you share today can be nurtured into a bridge that will enable you to journey over any of life's difficulties. The essence of love is self-giving; giving totally of yourselves to one another. Do not look so closely at how much your spouse will make you happy, will satisfy your needs, or ease your pain and discomfort. Rather, look at how you can give of yourself to your spouse. It is in this generous act of self-giving and in the generous acts of self-sacrifice that you will be made whole and your relationship will endure.

Important to your relationship with one another and to your marriage is a deep and abiding faith relationship with Christ Jesus. Christ Jesus will teach you the truly important things of life, especially the important things of married life. Remember always, dear *(Bride's Name)* and *(Groom's Name)*, that not only does Christ call us to "love one another" but, even more importantly, we are to love the Lord our God. And, with God, the longings of your hearts, the desires of your being, the gift of eternal love will be yours to have and to hold from this day forward.

Your journey together as husband and wife will undoubtedly be one of constant exploration and discovery: to discover one another in wonderful, new, and exciting ways; to grow with one another in faith, hope, and love; and to bring peace and joy to one another so that you may indeed live happily ever after.

(Bride's Name) and *(Groom's Name)*, may God perfect you in wisdom and in the love you share for one another that your days may be many and that you may truly live "happily ever after." God bless you both.

THE DOORWAY TO LOVE

(*Bride's Name*) and (*Groom's Name*), today you stand at a doorway; in fact, you stand on the very threshold of that doorway. As this door opens, you will enter a new and very different phase of your life's journey, and you enter it together, not alone. You are joining yourselves to each other today to become one, to enter a new doorway, and to embark to on this wonderful journey as husband and wife.

There is an old legend that dates back to early Roman times which says that the groom should carry the bride over the threshold of their home following the wedding ceremony. One explanation of this legend suggests that it was thought that if the bride was to stumble upon entering their home for the first time as a newlywed it would bring the couple bad luck and unhappy times for the duration of their married lives.

Whether you adhere to this old legend or not, I'm certain that with the faith that you both have shown for as long as I have known you, you will likely not stumble and fall. Though there may be times when you face uncertainties, difficult times, and the trials and tribulations that life brings through the doorways of our hearts and homes, an abiding faith in Christ Jesus will greatly aid in surmounting any obstacles which come your way.

As you open the doorway to your new lives together, be reminded that Christ Jesus desires to enter in and share with you. With Christ as a guest in your home and in your lives, your needs will be met, your lives blessed, and your love will grow in many wonderful and exciting ways. The Gospel of Matthew shares these familiar words:

> Ask, and it will be given you; search, and you will find; knock, and the door will be opened for you. For everyone who asks receives, and everyone who searches finds, and for everyone who knocks, the door will be opened. (7:7-8)

Simply put, these words are a subtle reminder that as you ask, search, and knock, Jesus, as your houseguest, will give to you in great abundance, help you find that which may be lost, and open the door to a dynamic faith journey, a journey that will bear much fruit because God cares for you and loves you beyond measure. Love one another in that same unselfish and reckless way.

(Bride's Name) and *(Groom's Name)*, while this message is quite brief, it exemplifies what I believe to be a profound sense of wisdom for you to learn by and live by. Keep the faith! Share the love! And most of all, invite the Lord God to be your guest in all your life together!

THERE IS LOVE

For a Service of Renewal of Vows

Therefore a man leaves his father and his mother and clings to his wife, and they become one flesh. (Genesis 2:24)

"There is love," say the many poets and writers in a multitude of ways, but I think Noel Paul Stookey says it best in his song by the same name. Stookey has noted that he based this popular wedding song on Matthew 18:20: "For where two or three are gathered in my name, I am there among them." In this love song he also poses the immensely profound question, "What's to be the reason for becoming man and wife? Is it love that brings you here, or love that brings you life?"

I would venture to guess that the answer to the first question is a resounding "Yes!" Love has certainly brought you here; it's the single most important reason for becoming husband and wife. It was God's gift of love that also brought you to life. And always remember, *(Bride's Name)* and *(Groom's Name)*, that it was the love of your parents—through God's blessings—that brought you to life and enabled you both to be here with us today.

It is clear that it is the great love that you share, the way you care for each other, the very special gleam in your eyes, and the passion of friendship that you nurture that have brought you here on this momentous occasion. Without your love for one another, without the love that your parents have shared with you through the years, and without God's love firmly rooted in your lives, it is highly unlikely that you would be standing before us today. It is in the coming together, the merging of all of this love, friendship, and passion that mark the reason for your becoming husband and wife.

Love is certainly the very foundation of marriage, yet marriage does not actually begin with the statement of vows or the exchange of rings. A wedding, in many ways, is a public declaration of a commitment already entered into by the couple. In other words, a wedding ceremony is a public unveiling of a marriage already in progress. Your love has been growing and maturing for quite some time now, and many of us here today have been witnesses to this lovely romantic transformation which has been taking place in your lives.

May the Spirit of God continue to work in the merging of your lives. May the Spirit of God continue to bless you with a transformation that brings about peace, joy, and continued love. Blessed be the God who embraces us all in the shelter of happiness and holiness.

RENEWING YOUR VOWS

(Wife's Name) and *(Husband's Name)*, your lives have been joined together in marriage for *(number of years)* years now. No doubt you are wondering how those years slipped by so quickly. But in that time, I'm certain, you have learned so very much about each other. You have discovered many secrets about how to make a marriage relationship grow and survive through all the difficult times that life presents. And, yes, you have experienced many of the joys and rewards that are meant for a husband and wife.

One of the wonderful things that I have experienced as I have come to know you both over the years is how, while you have become one in marriage, you are still two unique individuals. In becoming "one" in marriage, you have also allowed yourselves to become more fully your own identifiable selves. I honestly believe that this is God's desire for the institution of marriage: to be one in love, yet remain individual personalities.

(Wife's Name) and *(Husband's Name)*, you have loved much as well. One of the great joys that you have shared with me are the stories of your family stories of raising children who deeply care for and love you. Because of your love for one another, the love you share with your family and the love that you extend to so many others in this faith community and beyond, truly identifies you as a bright light that shines in the world today. In a world that seems so darkened by fractured relationships and broken marriages, you *(Wife's Name)* and *(Husband's Name)* give meaning and substance to marriage and togetherness.

It is certainly a joy and an honor to be with you here today as you celebrate *(number of years)* years of married life and profess to one another and to God your continuing love and devotion to one another. *(Wife's Name)* and *(Husband's Name)*, the story of your marriage offers a much better sermon than I could ever hope to preach this day. You are by God's amazing grace living, breathing examples of what is right in the world today.

As you both renew your vows today, I urge you to recall all of those joyous and wonderful feelings of your wedding day. Recall the reasons for your success. Recall how you have shared your wisdom in counseling other couples embarking on their journey together. Recall how God has blessed you in abundant ways. And believe that your future will be even more blessed than your past. Thanks be to God.

REDEEMING LOVE

(Bride's Name) and *(Groom's Name)*, today you embark on a new venture in marriage. It is a second marriage for both of you and I know there have been concerns and questions raised. Let

me tell you today that God is good in all things. One of the many names we use to address God is Redeemer, and aren't we all glad! God loves each and every one of us and gives us second chances in many, many areas—including marriage.

While marriage is intended "until we are parted by death," divorce is one of the painful tragedies that humans sometimes experience; it is certainly an unfortunate rupture or breaking of a promise or covenant. As Christians, however, we trust in God's redeeming love and our human capacity to be healed and made whole once again. The failure of a commitment does not mean that God will foreclose on other attempts at expressing love and grace.

Simply put, God offers second chances when we have the courage and faith to ask for them. Those second chances occur in the present, but they include baggage and ghosts of our past. Actually, reminders and memories are present in all marriages— whether a second marriage or a first marriage. Everyone has their own unique quirks, habits, and past failures; in new relationships, we must learn to deal with them in a positive manner.

I believe your marriage will succeed because you have expressed a heartfelt desire and commitment to communicate fully and openly. Your willingness to communicate in this man- ner and work through any disagreements is vital to a marriage's success. As you work as partners journeying through life together, give one another a measure of privacy, respect, and support. Be generous and offer one another tender, loving care. Share your hopes, dreams, and visions for the future. Be as forgiving as God is—that is, share with one another a sense and spirit of redeem- ing love.

(Bride's Name) and (Groom's Name), it is vitally important that you discover—together—God's design and purpose for your second marriage. God will offer you many, many opportunities to succeed and I encourage you to make God an integral and impor- tant component of your marriage.

Be realistic. Marriage, while offering you numerous joys and moments for celebration, will also have its difficult days. It can be hard work, but the effort will certainly be worth it.

Please remember that you are not alone in this venture. There is always a Divine Power present to uphold you and to give you strength, focus, and encouragement as needed. God has a special ministry for you both as you witness to your faith and serve as examples for others. Be a blessing to one another, be a blessing to God, and be a blessing to all who see your love blossom and grow.

WEDDING
INFORMATION FORM

Bride

Full Name: _____

Address: _____

City: _____ State: _____ Zip: _____

Phone: (home) _____ (work) _____

E-mail: _____ (mobile) _____

Date of Birth: _____ Current Age: _____

Previously Married? _____ Any Children? _____

If yes, children's names and ages:

_____

Your Parents' Names and Addresses:

_____

_____

Current Church Membership: _____

Church Address: _____

City: _____ State: _____ Zip: _____

If not currently a member of a church, in what faith were you raised (or do you actively practice)?

_____

Groom

Full Name: _____

Address: _____

City: _____ State: _____ Zip: _____

Phone: (home) _____ (work) _____

E-mail: _____ (mobile) _____

Date of Birth: _____ Current Age: _____

Previously Married? _____ Any Children? _____

If yes, children's names and ages:

_____

Your Parents' Names and Addresses:

_____

_____

Current Church Membership: _____

Church Address: _____

City: _____ State: _____ Zip: _____

If not currently a member of a church, in what faith were you raised (or do you actively practice)?

_____

Arrangement Details

Wedding Date: _____ Time: _____

Rehearsal Date: _____ Time: _____

Wedding Party Information

Presenter: Relationship:

_____   _____

Maid / Matron of Honor: Best Man:

_____   _____

Attendants: Groomsmen:

_____   _____

_____   _____

_____   _____

_____   _____

Flower Girl: Ring Bearer:

_____   _____

Outside Musicians (if any) and special music desired (selections are subject to pastoral approval):

_____

_____

Do you desire to celebrate Communion? _____

Do you desire a sermon or meditation? _____

Favorite Bible passages: Scripture Reader(s):

_____   _____

Unity Candle? _____   (Couple to provide the unity candle and 2 taper candles)

Other ritual(s) desired:

_____

APPENDIX B

PASTOR'S WEDDING POLICY STATEMENT

Congratulations on your decision to be married at *(Name of Church)*. This is an important day for you, and this statement has been prepared to help you plan and prepare for your wedding service. While this policy statement cannot anticipate each and every situation, please know that I am flexible and will work with you to ensure a joyous, personalized wedding celebration.

Marriage is ordained by God as a gift for men and women. As such, marriage is viewed as a lifelong commitment to be shared with one another. I would encourage you to remember the old adage that "A wedding is just one day, but a marriage is for a lifetime." Any wedding service should be considered first and foremost a worship service; it is a joyous occasion to seek God's blessing for the years ahead.

Couples intending to be married at *(Name of Church)* Church are strongly urged to attend our Sunday worship services at least four consecutive Sundays prior to the wedding date.

DATES

All dates must be approved by the pastor before a wedding can be scheduled. It is important that sufficient time be allowed to guarantee a wedding date.

INVOLVEMENT OF OTHER CLERGY

If a clergyperson from another church is desired to be a part of the wedding service, the invitation must come from the host pastor. The role of outside clergy is left to the discretion of the presiding pastor. Likewise, if I am requested to be a part of your wedding service at another church, that invitation must come from the host pastor of that church.

PREMARRIAGE COUNSELING

All couples must participate in premarital counseling as a part of the process. This counseling will involve a discussion of the couple's strengths and weaknesses and their marriage goals. Time will also be devoted to discussing the wedding liturgy and planning the service.

DIVORCE / PREGNANCY

If the bride-to-be is pregnant or if either party has been divorced, I would appreciate knowing about it up front. This does not mean I will not perform the ceremony; I would simply like to have such information beforehand.

ALCOHOL / DRUG USE

Please be aware that if the use of alcohol or drugs is evident prior to the start of the wedding service, I will not be able to perform the ceremony. It is possible that the service may be able to be rescheduled to a later date.

HONORARIUM

The current pastoral fee for performing a wedding service is
$*(amount)*, and the fee must be paid at least two weeks prior to
the wedding service. The fee includes time spent with the couple
in counseling, preparation of the wedding service liturgy, the
wedding rehearsal, and the conduct of the actual wedding service. This fee, however, is nonrefundable in the unlikely event
that the wedding service is cancelled.

This fee is waived for persons who are active in the life of (*Name
of Church*) Church.

JUST IN TIME!

The JUST IN TIME! series offers brief, practical resources
of immediate help for pastors at an affordable price.